UNDERSTANDING

THE
BROODMARE

YOUR **GUIDE** TO HORSE HEALTH
CARE AND MANAGEMENT

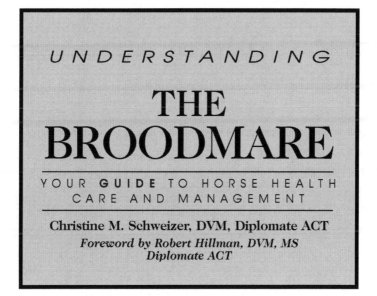

UNDERSTANDING

THE
BROODMARE

YOUR **GUIDE** TO HORSE HEALTH
CARE AND MANAGEMENT

Christine M. Schweizer, DVM, Diplomate ACT

Foreword by Robert Hillman, DVM, MS
Diplomate ACT

ECLIPSE PRESS

Essex, Connecticut

An imprint of Globe Pequot, the trade division of
The Rowman & Littlefield Publishing Group, Inc.
4501 Forbes Blvd., Ste. 200
Lanham, MD 20706
www.rowman.com

Distributed by NATIONAL BOOK NETWORK

British Library Cataloguing in Publication Information available

Library of Congress Cataloging-in-Publication Data Available

ISBN 978-1-4930-7474-7 (pbk. : alk. paper)

∞™ The paper used in this publication meets the minimum
requirements of American National Standard for Information
Sciences—Permanence of Paper for Printed Library Materials,
ANSI/NISO Z39.48-1992.

Contents

FOREWORD

The first International Symposium on Equine Reproduction held in 1974 at Cambridge, U.K. brought together the leading researchers in equine reproduction from all over the world. Discussions at this meeting served as a catalyst and stimulated a great increase in research studies on all phases of equine reproduction. While these studies are continuing at an increasingly sophisticated level, they have already produced a tremendous amount of new information that has permitted many improvements in broodmare management and therapeutic protocols. When properly used, the incorporation of this newer information has produced increased conception and foaling rates, which in turn resulted in a larger, healthier foal crop. However, much of this information has been published in diverse and fragmented sources.

In *Understanding The Broodmare* and in the upcoming companion text *Understanding Breeding Management*, Dr. Christine Schweizer has pulled this new information together and combined it with the wisdom of her considerable clinical experience. The result is a well-organized, easily followed text that is carefully indexed so that the reader can quickly locate an area of concern and extract the latest techniques to address the problem.

In *Understanding The Broodmare* the management of the pregnant and foaling mare is fully discussed. Throughout the texts, in addition to discussing therapeutic options to be used when problems occur, Dr. Schweizer emphasizes management procedures that can be employed to prevent these problems.

Dr. Schweizer has done an extraordinary job of bringing together a large volume of information and condensing and organizing it in a coherent and easily readable manner. The information in *Understanding Breeding Management* and *Understanding The Broodmare* is current and complete. These two books will be valuable assets to the seasoned broodmare manager seeking the newest techniques and therapies as well as a complete "how to" manual for the neophyte broodmare owner.

Robert Hillman, DVM, MS
Diplomate ACT
Senior Clinician Emeritus, NYSCVM
Cornell University

INTRODUCTION

I was in my freshman year of undergraduate studies at Cornell University's College of Agriculture and Life Sciences when I observed my first foaling. I had grown up around Thoroughbred racehorses on the backstretches of Belmont Park and Saratoga Racecourse in New York, where my grandfather had spent the majority of his life galloping and grooming racehorses. My grandfather's profound love for the equine had skipped a generation and landed squarely in my heart. When I was a young girl, my grandfather would take me to visit his charges and ride the stable ponies. My grandfather died during my freshman year of veterinary school. I miss him, but I still feel his love for me and the horses he taught me so much about.

As I grew, my desire to be around horses every waking moment became difficult for books, pictures, and weekend outings to satisfy. I can never truly describe the gift given to me by the horsemen and owners of Strapro Racing Stable, who used to summer at Belmont Park and mentored a young girl as she walked hots and groomed stable ponies. My happiest days have been spent learning to apply poultices and wrap legs while listening to racing stories and words of wisdom and horsemanship given generously to me by grooms and exercise boys on sunny, summer mornings in the shedrow of Barn 34.

As a teenager, I went to work as a veterinary assistant for Dr. Harry "Hap" Hemphill, who had a racetrack practice at Belmont Park and Saratoga and a farm on Long Island. I spent many hours cleaning and stocking trucks and offices, and holding horses and eq uipmenht while Dr. Hemphill worked. It was a joyous time for me, and further fueled my desire to become a veterinarian.

When I arrived at Cornell as an undergraduate, I was instantly drawn to the Animal Science Department and immediately switched my major from biology to animal science. The Veterinary College's section of theriogenology (reproductive medicine) maintains a teaching band of broodmares at the university horse farm, and every spring all interested undergraduates are invited to participate in the nightwatch. The trade off for a missed night's sleep was the opportunity to be on hand for a foaling. Although I had tried to be present for foalings on Hap's farm, I had never been successful. My horse crazy dorm mates, Kate and Sue, and I jumped at the chance. (The activity was dubbed "the fool watch" by less enthusiastic individuals!) Finally, Kate and I were rewarded for our efforts. On that particular evening, the mares had been quiet and peaceful and were giving no indication that anything exciting might be afoot. About 1 a.m., Kate left the office to check on the mares and quickly returned to say that a mare named Top Jezzy seemed to be breaking her water. She returned to watch as I excitedly phoned Dr. Robert Hillman, the veterinarian in charge of the mares. Dr. Hillman had lectured all of us foal watchers on what to expect in a normal foaling and what to do in an emergency. He was and is a roll model to all of us and has had a profound effect on me and my career as a veterinarian.

When I got off the phone with Dr. Hillman, I hurried to join Kate watching the mare. It became quickly apparent from what Dr. Hillman had taught us to expect that Top Jezzy's foaling was not progressing normally. Only one of the foal's front feet had appeared after several minutes of straining, and it seemed that the foal must be malpositioned. Dr. Hillman arrived within a few minutes, and calmly took charge of the situation. He corrected the foal's position (she had one leg back and was speedily repositioned) as Kate and I assisted him, and delivered the foal. The foal was very vigorous despite its shaky entrance into the world and began sucking on Dr. Hillman's chin after taking a few breaths. As I heard Dr. Hillman quietly murmur, "I love you, too," to the foal, I was mesmerized by the scene and knew I wouldn't be happy unless I could spend my life doing the same.

There have been quite a few foalings since that night, and each has been special in its own way. The magic of horses and horse people is that each and every one has something new to teach you, and life is incredibly full and joyous. Special thanks to the horsemen, veterinarians, and instructors who carried me on my path, as well as my family. I also thank my husband, Dr. Joseph Wilder, and our daughters Caylan and Falynn, whose love and support fill my heart and inspire my days.

When I set out to write *Understanding The Broodmare*, I did so with the hope that I might address a few of the problems and questions I frequently encounter in broodmare practice, and in so doing help mare owners have a better understanding of their mares and the events that overtake them. It is important, and I think enjoyable, for mare owners and managers to have an understanding of the mare's normal reproductive cycles, behaviors, and physiology to better understand and work with the daily events in a broodmare's life. Once you know what the normal looks like, it is easier to recognize the abnormal and seek a veterinarian's help.

I hope after reading this book, the mare owner will also have a greater feeling for the "whys" behind many of the management practices and treatments a veterinarian might recommend for an individual mare and be more comfortable making decisions for their mares. I hope that the following pages contain information that will be useful to both the novice and the experienced broodmare owner. The knowledge offered within this book is not intended, however, to replace a veterinarian's "hands on" advice and expertise.

Mares, as you will read, are individuals. Although all follow the reproductive script of their species, each puts her own spin on the whole breeding and foaling process. The only concrete rule I have found to date is that they can't get pregnant if you don't put semen into them! Enjoy the process and roll with the difficulties if you can. Take stock during the process and never forget to pause for a moment and enjoy the work and the horses you are blessed with. May you be a blessing to them as well.

Christine M. Schweizer, DVM,
Diplomate ACT
Cornell University
Ithaca, New York

CHAPTER 1

The Pregnant Mare

The pregnant mare has "treasure in her belly"
— A Bedouin saying

The role of the broodmare on any farm is to produce a live, healthy foal, and thereby pass her genes on to a new generation of horses. All of an owner's hopes and management efforts culminate in that hour when the mare begins to labor to deliver her foal, and success is measured in the foal's first breaths and unsteady steps. In the wild, the mare must rely on her strength, condition, experience, instinct, and luck to deliver her foal and the placenta, to see that the foal nurses that first, vital colostrum, and to bond with the foal so that it recognizes and follows her. Failure to accomplish any of these tasks could result in the death of the foal and even the mare.

The foal's initial strength and vitality also determine the outcome, as the foal plays an active role in its own birth and survival right from the beginning. When considering the potential for disaster at almost every point in this scenario, along with the fact that mares have been delivering foals on their own for eons, it becomes apparent that Nature knows what she is doing. Intervention by humans, on the other hand, actually can be counterproductive.

Having said that, it is also important to recognize that our domestic environment imposes conditions (such as concentration of disease pathogens) that can interfere with or create problems for the broodmare and her foal. Those who undertake the responsibility of managing the foaling mare must learn to recognize what is normal and what is not, to identify potential problems, and troubleshoot. Planning and preparedness can help prevent illness or loss of the mare and foal.

The wild mare has no choice but to rely ultimately on luck. It is best for the domestic mare that her caretakers leave as little to luck as possible. Otherwise, all of the time, effort, and money that went into bringing the mare to this moment of delivery may have been for nothing.

PREGNANCY PHYSIOLOGY

Fertilization of the mare's ovulated egg (oocyte) by the stallion's sperm occurs in the mare's oviducts (uterine tubes). For the first five to six days after ovulation, the developing equine embryo is nourished and supported by the oviduct. During this period, the embryo is dividing so that by the time it reaches the uterus on the fifth or sixth day after ovulation it has grown from a single-cell embryo to a multi-cell embryo (late morali or early

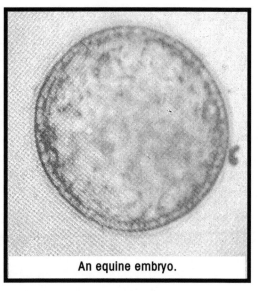

An equine embryo.

blastocyst stage) still surrounded by a protective coat (the zona pellucida).

The mare's oviducts can distinguish between viable

embryos and unfertilized oocytes. How they are able to make this distinction is unclear. With few exceptions, only developing embryos enter the uterus. Unfertilized eggs are retained within the oviduct where they degenerate over time.

The embryo undergoes rapid growth and expansion upon entering the uterus. The expanding blastocyst "hatches" from its zona pellucida about eight days after ovulation. After hatching, the embryo is still surrounded by a protective glycoprotein coating that formed underneath the zona pellucida. This coating, the capsule, is thought to provide mechanical protection and support to the embryo; it also might protect the embryo against any organisms that still might be infecting the uterus.

The embryo is mobile within the uterus for the first 15 to 17 days after ovulation. The capsule likely helps the embryo maintain its spherical shape and prevents the embryo from becoming damaged as it traverses the lumen of the uterine horns and body. The embryo's diameter greatly increases during this time. By 10 days after ovulation, the embryo has grown from the microscopic so much that on ultrasound it will be about 3 millimeters (mm) in diameter, and by 15 days it will be 15 to 20 mm in diameter.

The mobility of the equine embryo within the uterus for such a long time after ovulation is one of its unique features. The embryo journeys back and forth throughout the uterine lumen from the time of its arrival in the uterus until it "fixes" in the base of one of the uterine horns usually by day 15 to 17 after ovulation. It is thought that this mobility is necessary for maternal recognition of pregnancy. In the cycling, non-pregnant mare, the uterus normally will produce prostaglandin on the 14th day after ovulation to terminate the progesterone-producing corpus luteum on the ovary. In this way the diestrus period is brought to an end, and the mare cycles back into estrus to begin a new cycle and another chance to become pregnant. If the mare is pregnant, however, it is vital that the corpus luteum (CL) be maintained so that progesterone production by the ovary (which is vital to the maintenance of the early equine pregnancy) is not interrupted or terminated. Maternal recognition of pregnancy is the event by which the equine embryo signals the uterus that it is present and prevents the endometrium from producing prostaglandin. The mechanism by which the embryo signals the endometrium is not clearly understood, although it likely involves the production of an embryonic product. What is understood, however, is that the embryo must take this message to the entire surface area of the uterine lumen; otherwise, the endometrium will produce prostaglandin, and the pregnancy will be lost. Therefore, anything that obstructs embryonic movement or in any other way interferes with the signaling process will likely result in termination of the pregnancy.

The embryo migrates frequently from one end of the uterus to the other during a 24-hour period. This movement picks up in intensity between days 11 to 14 so that the embryo is likely covering the entire surface area of the endometrium every few hours. The embryo's movement through the uterine horns and body is facilitated by uterine contraction, which is likely further modulated by direct signaling from the embryo.

By day 15 to 17, the embryo comes to rest in the base of one of the uterine horns, becoming "fixed" in this location. The embryo has continued to grow (usually it is about 2.5 centimeters (cm) by day 17) and the increase in uterine tone effectively decreases the size of the uterine lumen so that the growing embryo becomes "stuck." Embryos that are the result of foal heat matings almost always become fixed in the smaller, previously non-pregnant horn. Those few pregnancies that fixate in the uterine body as opposed to the horns seem to be lost at a higher frequency than "horn pregnancies."

Once the embryo fixates it continues to develop, and the embryonic vesicle loses its spherical appearance about 19 to

20 days after ovulation. At this point it takes on an irregular outline that conforms to the uterine folds. This change corresponds to the loss of the glycoprotein capsule. By day 21 to 22, the embryo proper starts to become visible in the bottom of the fluid-filled vesicle, and by day 23 to 25 an embryonic heartbeat first becomes discernible on ultrasound as a tiny flicker.

On ultrasound, the fluid-filled chamber above the embryo proper is the embryonic yolk sack that has helped nourish the embryo. Beginning around day 23, the developing allantois becomes visible as a line suspending the embryo from

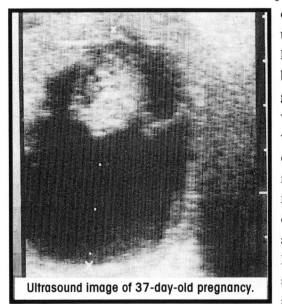

Ultrasound image of 37-day-old pregnancy.

one side of the vesicle to the other. This membrane line starts out along the bottom of the vesicle and gradually migrates upwardly through the vesicle as the allantois expands and the yolk sack regresses. The expanding fluid cavity below the embryo is the developing allantoic placental cavity. By 28 days the embryo is suspended in an equatorial position by the allantoic membrane, and by 36 days the allantoic cavity and membrane has expanded so that the embryo is now hanging from the "roof" of the fluid-filled embryonic vesicle. The yolk sack disappears as the umbilical cord forms, and the embryo gradually descends toward the bottom of the vesicle. Diameterwise the vesicle has expanded very little between days 20 and 30 compared with its expansion between days 10 and 20, but the size of the pregnancy continues to increase so that on rectal palpation it is 3 to 5 cm in diameter by about 30 days and about 8 cm by about 45 days. The changes in size and sequential orientation of the pregnancy as the embryo first "ascends" and then "descends" through the vesicle, as well as the presence of a heartbeat at the expected time, are helpful in both assessing how old the pregnancy is and whether it is developing at an expected rate. In my experience, many embryonic losses after day 18 seem to occur sometime between day 20 and day 25 and are first recognizable as such by the fact that the embryo proper and/or its heartbeat fail to appear at the expected times. Also, embryos that fail to take on the normal alignment (i.e., arise from the side or "roof" of the vesicle initially as opposed to the "floor") also seem to be at a higher risk for loss than normally aligned embryos.

Implantation of the equine embryo does not occur until nearly day 40 of gestation. Implantation is when the uterus and fetal membranes begin to attach to one another and direct exchange of nutrients and waste products between the mare's and the developing foal's circulatory systems begins to occur. The horse is unique in that the embryo remains "unattached" for such a long period of time during early pregnancy and relies on the histotroph (uterine milk) produced by the uterine glands for its nourishment and support. It is easy to understand, therefore, why mares which have damaged uterine endometriums with large amounts of fibrosis "choking off" the uterine glands have a more difficult time maintaining an embryo.

The "mature" equine placenta has a diffuse attachment of microcotyledons (tufts of finger-like microvilli) that interlock with the uterine endometrium over its entire surface area so that there is a 1:1 exchange of nutrients. The expansion and attachment of the fetal membranes has a slow and tenuous beginning at around day 40 with the first villi forming an attachment with the uterus at the base of the pregnant horn. The membranes gradually expand to cover the entire uterine lumen by about day 75, but the microvilli's attachment to the endometrium is not fully developed until 100 or more days.

As the attachment becomes stronger and nutrient exchange increases, the role of the glandular histotroph becomes less important.

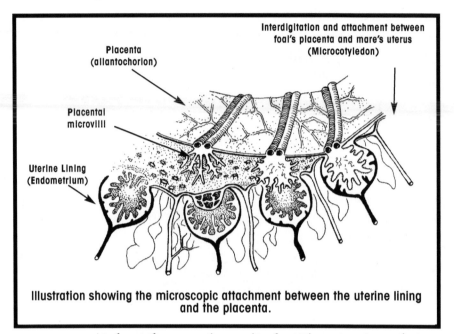

Illustration showing the microscopic attachment between the uterine lining and the placenta.

At about the same time as implantation, structures that are unique to the equine placenta — the endometrial cups — begin to form. These cups are important because they produce the hormone equine chorionic gonadotropin that causes the formation of secondary corpora lutea on the ovaries. These corpora lutea serve as backup to the primary corpus luteum that formed at ovulation to ensure that the mare's ovaries continue to produce enough progesterone to maintain the pregnancy until the placenta assumes pregnancy maintenance at approximately 120 to 150 days of gestation. The endometrial cups are formed from embryonic trophoblast cells that migrate from the chorionic girdle of the embryo into the endometrium of the mare at about 35 days of gestation. The trophoblast cells become embedded as aggregates of cells in the wall of the endometrium, and begin producing equine chorionic gonadotropin.

Once formed, the endometrial cups will persist and function, regardless of whether the pregnancy is still viable, until they are rejected by the mare's immune system. The mare normally will not return to estrus while the cups are functioning. The mare's immune system begins to reject the cups around 60-80 days of the gestation, and they are usually gone by 120 days. Equine chorionic gonadotropin levels are detectable beginning about day 40, peak around day 60 to 70, and are low usually by day 100 but still detectable sometimes until about day 120 to 150.

CHAPTER 2

Pregnancy Diagnosis

In general, pregnant mares will fail to return to behavioral estrus as expected 17 to 19 days following ovulation, and will reject the advances of a teaser. However, failure to return to estrus does not ensure that a mare has a viable pregnancy. Horses experience a relatively high percentage of early embryonic loss, and many mares might have had an embryo or embryonic remnants that were able to signal their presence successfully to the uterus at the time of maternal recognition of pregnancy, but were no longer viable a few days later. Therefore, these mares still would have an active corpus luteum (CL) and fail to return to estrus. There also is a percentage of mares which will experience a second ovulation during mid to late diestrus (greater than or equal to day 10 after the first ovulation) and still have a second, active CL at 21 days even though the first CL is no longer present. (The mare's endometrium still produces prostaglandin 14 days after the first ovulation, which eliminates the first CL, but the second CL is too young to respond to the prostaglandin and so persists.)

Likewise, teasing behavior as an indicator of pregnancy status cannot be relied upon in mares which regularly do not show heat well. On the flip side, some pregnant mares will display signs of estrus if they develop a large follicle. Typically this will occur around 18 to 20 days of gestation (right when you would expect an open mare to return to her next heat cycle), but these mares usually will tease half-heartedly. They might stand somewhat quietly and raise their tails and even wink, but they usually do not break down well for the teaser, and object vigorously to being mounted. Attempting a live mating with a mare like this is dangerous for her, the stallion, and their handlers. The estrogen being produced by the large follicle causes this mild positive response, but in the end the progesterone being excreted by the primary pregnancy CL makes her say NO! I have seen pregnant mares demonstrate this lukewarm teasing at later points in gestation, usually around 35 to 50 days, when the mares have multiple follicles that are destined to become secondary CLs. On palpation, however, these pregnant mares (especially at 18 to 20 days) will have tremendous uterine tone and a very tight cervix, indicating an active CL. In some cases a pregnancy bulge at 20 days might be palpable as well, and if examined by ultrasound the pregnancy is readily discernible. If artificial insemination is being used, it is important that the mare be examined thoroughly for pregnancy before being rebred so that an established pregnancy is not lost when the cervix is violated and semen is dumped on top of the developing embryo. If the cervix is tight in an estrus mare which has been previously bred, double-check to be sure she is not pregnant before attempting to breed her!

Lastly, there is that group of mares which short-cycle themselves before the 18th day after ovulation. Usually this occurs because the mare has developed a uterine infection and is

AT A GLANCE

• Direct rectal palpation by a veterinarian can verify a mare's pregnancy status.

• Ultrasound can identify a pregnancy as early as 10 days after ovulation.

• Twins which survive to birth are usually small and weak.

• Mares which double ovulate usually do so repeatedly.

trying to clear it by coming into heat early. This early estrus could have been missed if the mare was not teased after ovulation or examined prior to 18 days by a veterinarian trying to detect an early pregnancy (10 to 18 days after ovulation) with

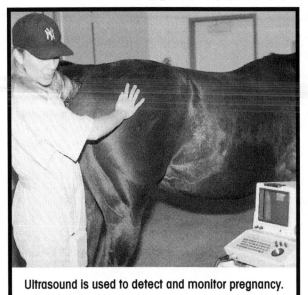

Ultrasound is used to detect and monitor pregnancy.

an ultrasound examination. These mares already might have a new CL established or forming at what would have been 18 to 20 days from the observed previous estrus and therefore will also not show heat at the previously expected time.

Direct rectal palpation of the mare's reproductive tract by an experienced veterinarian can verify a mare's pregnancy status. Changes in the mare's uterine tone (which is quite tubular during early pregnancy, especially around 18 to 20 days) and increased, firm cervical tone indicate early on that the mare might be pregnant. The embryo itself becomes palpable as a ventral bulge in the base of the pregnant horn as early as 18 to 20 days in some mares (maiden mares usually) and reliably in most mares by 25 to 30 days of gestation.

The age of the pregnancy can be roughly estimated in days up until about 90 days by palpation. After that time the uterus is over the brim of the mare's pelvis and its true size not readily discernible. However, finding that the cervix is closed and pulled forward and the uterus has a normal resilient tone and is enlarged and fluid-filled all still indicate to the palpation that the mare is pregnant. The fetus becomes readily palpable after four months of gestation provided it is not lying too deeply in the abdomen. As pregnancy advances, the fetus cannot "hide" and will be readily palpable to the veterinarian.

The palpable size of the pregnancy relative to the breeding or ovulation dates indicate to the experienced veterinarian whether the pregnancy appears to be progressing normally. Pregnancies that are small for gestational age can indicate pregnancy loss and warrant further investigation either by serial palpations, or by ultrasound to definitively diagnose the viability of an embryo or fetus. Pregnancies that seem larger than they should be, or where bulges are discovered in the base of both horns, are immediately suspect for twin pregnancies and warrant examination using an ultrasound machine. Once the fetus is palpable, the presence of spontaneous movement indicates to the veterinarian that the fetus is literally "alive and kicking."

Lack of fetal movement in an otherwise palpable fetus does not necessarily mean there is a problem (sometimes the foal is asleep), but failure to find or elicit movement (or the finding that the foal is hyperactive) after several minutes of assessment could indicate a problem and should be investigated. Changes in uterine tone quality at any point also can signal a problem. The tone of the uterine horns early on should be pronounced and tubular. Later, as the uterus becomes distended with the fetal membranes, fetus and fluids, the pregnant uterus is resilient and somewhat thin-walled. Except at the very end of pregnancy, the cervix should be pronounced and tight with no edema or softening. Once the foal itself is palpable, the uterus should be soft and pliant and not thickened or tightly distended with fluids. Any findings that differ from the norm indicate there might be a problem.

Veterinary ultrasound examination has been a boon to broodmare practice. When used to detect and monitor pregnancy, it offers management advantages that cannot be implemented when using teasing and/or palpation alone to determine a mare's status.

First, ultrasound examination can identify a pregnancy as

early as 10 days and reliably by 14 days after ovulation. The obvious advantage to early detection is confirming that the mare carried an early embryo to this point; ultrasound also lets the veterinarian interpret the status of the pregnancy. The embryo should appear perfectly round and be a characteristic diameter for a given day after ovulation. From time to time it might be difficult for a veterinarian to determine if the fluid-filled structure he or she is examining within the uterine lumen is an embryo or an endometrial cyst. In general, cysts will not be perfectly round and they will appear to be "off center," but sometimes it can be hard to tell. A cyst, however, is stationary and will not grow appreciably over a one- to three-day period, and so, when in doubt, serial examinations might be necessary. If the embryo is undersized for gestational age or has an abnormal contour, or if there is edema or free fluid in the uterus, the risk for early pregnancy loss is greater.

Simultaneous assessment of palpable tone of the reproductive structures also can indicate how well the pregnancy is developing. A small embryo or decreased uterine tone does not necessarily mean the pregnancy is in trouble, but it does warrant closer monitoring. Examining the mare before the 18th day after ovulation also identifies those mares which are not pregnant and assesses the status of the ovarian structures and tubular tract changes so that the next cycle is not missed and the mare can be promptly bred again. It also offers the chance to identify those mares which might retain a CL and require prostaglandin therapy to bring them back into estrus in a timely fashion. A note of caution here: In my experience, it is always best to delay giving prostaglandin if there is any chance the mare might have a viable but undetected pregnancy. Some mares do not have a demonstrable embryo at 14 days after ovulation, but when a follow-up examination is performed within the next four days (or if the mare fails to return to heat) a small but viable embryo is found and the mare often goes on to have a normal pregnancy. Treating too hastily with prostaglandin will terminate this pregnancy.

Probably the greatest advantage of using rectal ultrasound for determining pregnancy is the early detection of twin pregnancies. Twin pregnancies that persist past 40 or more days rarely end successfully. The majority of them end in abortion sometime during the late second or third trimester, or produce dead or small, weak foals at term. Detecting twins before the embryos are fixed in the base of one or both horns allows for more options for reducing the twin pregnancy to a singleton before the endometrial cups form. Lastly, ultrasound offers a chance to monitor serially the viability of a pregnancy during the early stages right on up to foaling (after 70 to 90 days the foal's heartbeat is imaged across the mare's abdomen). It is a definite advantage to be able to monitor a pregnancy for the first 35 to 40 days to detect the loss of an embryo in a timely fashion so a previously pregnant mare with a persistent CL is not permitted to go open unnoticed as the days of the breeding season tick away.

Measurement of progesterone, equine chorionic gonadotropin, and estrone sulfate in the blood of pregnant mares at specific periods during the gestation also can be useful to equine pregnancy diagnosis. Blood hormone testing could be particularly useful in those situations when rectal examination cannot be performed safely (extremely uncooperative mare, or mare which is physically too small to be examined by a given examiner, e.g., some miniature mares). Progesterone levels are NOT specific for pregnancy. All an elevated blood progesterone level means is that there is an active CL(s) somewhere on the ovary. It gives no information as to whether there is also a viable pregnancy. If, however, progesterone levels are low (less than 1 nanogram per milliliter (ml)) at 18 to 20 days after the last ovulation, it is likely the mare is not pregnant. If progesterone levels are elevated, the mare indeed might be pregnant, but further examination will be necessary to confirm it.

Equine chorionic gonadotropin (ECG) is produced by the endometrial cups. This hormone can be detected beginning at 35 to 40 days of gestation, with levels peaking sometime around 60 to 70 days, then declining (as the cups are rejected by the mare's immune system) to undetectable levels by days 100 to 150. The presence of ECG in the mare's blood between days 40 to 100 and beyond indicates that the mare had a viable pregnancy at least at the 35- to 40-day mark. Remember, the endometrial cups will function for their set period regardless of whether the pregnancy is lost.

The live fetal-placental unit produces estrogen during pregnancy. Fetal estrogen production is reflected by increasing levels of estrone sulfate in the mare's blood and urine detectable after 60 to 90 days of gestation (peak levels occur at about 210 days). If the fetus dies, estrogen production ceases, and the estrone sulfate levels drop precipitously. Therefore, measurement of elevated blood or urine estrone sulfate levels after 60 to 90 days positively identifies the presence of a viable pregnancy. The main disadvantage of using this method of diagnosing pregnancy is that the levels do not become significant until later on during gestation.

The following recommended schedule for detecting and monitoring pregnancy in mares summarizes and addresses the points we have discussed.

Number of Days Post Ovulation	Procedure	Questions Looking to Answer
Day 14	Rectal palpation/ ultrasound; tease	Normal embryonic vesicle present? Twins? Quality of uterine and cervical tone? Normal diestrus appearance to uterus? What structures are present on the ovaries?
Day 18-20 (single check)	Rectal palpation/ ultrasound; tease	Normal embryonic vesicle Twins? Quality of tone and appearance

Number of Days Post Ovulation	Procedure	Questions Looking to Answer
		of uterus and cervix? If not pregnant, is she in heat or does the CL appear to be retained?
Day 25-30 (single check)	Rectal palpation/ ultrasound; tease	Normal embryo with a heartbeat? Twins? Quality of tone and appearance of uterus and cervix? If pregnancy is no longer present, has it been resorbed or are there still remnants visible? If not pregnant, is she in heat or does the CL appear to be retained?
Day 35-45 (single check)	Rectal palpation /ultrasound	Normal fetus with a heartbeat? Twins? Quality of tone and appearance of uterus and cervix? If pregnancy is no longer present, has it been resorbed or are there still remnants visible? Has she returned to heat or have secondary CLs already begun to form?
Day 60-80 (optional check unless the mare is being being supplemented) with progesterone)	Rectal palpation	Normal uterine and cervical tone? A palpable pregnancy that is the ap- appropriate size and distension for the state of gestation?
Day 100-120	Rectal palpation; ultrasound (optional)	Normal cervical tone? Uterine tone and distension normal for stage of gestation? Live foal? If being supplemented with progesterone, decision on whether to begin weaning the mare off needs to be made (usually starting at 120 days)

Depending on the finding at each evaluation, more frequent checks or further diagnostics might be needed. For
example, if a second, previously undetected CL is discovered
at the 14-day check, but only one embryo is detected at that
time, it might be prudent to check daily or every other day
between 14 and 20 days to look for a possible twin. Mares
on progesterone need to be checked more regularly between

35 and 120 days in the event that the fetus dies but abortion is prevented. In general, mares which are pregnant at 35 to 45 days are unlikely to cycle back if the pregnancy is lost until what would have been 90-plus days of gestation. Therefore, mares which are otherwise normal may not be looked at again until 100 days, but again, prompt detection of pregnancy loss will allow the mare to be managed so that she can be bred back as soon as she does begin cycling back.

The combination of teasing, rectal palpation, rectal ultra-sound, and blood hormone levels (when indicated) helps the veterinarian get an appreciation for the progress of the preg-nancy. A mare is never 100% "safe in foal," but the longer the gestation progresses the more established the foal becomes and the more likely it is to stay put. Obviously economics is a factor and the cost of frequent veterinary examinations must be weighed against the potential value (monetary and emo-tional) of the foal the mare is carrying and the cost of the mare coming up open at the end of the season.

MANAGEMENT OF TWIN PREGNANCIES

It is not an advantage to hope for "two for the price of one" when dealing with pregnant mares. While it seems that every person you meet has a tale about a mare which suc-cessfully delivered and raised twin foals, the truth is that the majority of equine twin pregnancies that survive beyond 40 days end in abortion during the second or third trimesters. The small percentage of twin foals which make it to birth are usually small and weak, and often one or both are born dead or die quickly despite of good nursing care and medical support.

Mares which deliver twin foals frequently have complicat-ed deliveries (foals become tangled during delivery and/or weak or dead foals are malpositioned), and frequently retain their placenta(s). Due to the trauma and resultant inflamma-tion (and sometimes infection) caused to the mare's repro-ductive tract by the late-term abortions, it is typically difficult to get the mare bred back in the subsequent breeding season. This means two years are lost in the mare's reproductive life, and it is potentially three to four years from the time she first conceived the twins until she carries a viable, singleton pregnancy to term and a foal hits the ground.

The reason horses are not usually successful carrying twins to term has to do with the equine's placentation. As we have discussed, attachment and nutrient exchange between the foal's placenta and the mare's uterus is accomplished in a 1:1 ratio. If two foals occupy the space originally designed for one, the best case scenario is that they share the uterus 50-50, but this still means each foal is receiving only half the support and nutrient exchange it would receive if it was the only foal. If, as in most twin pregnancies, there is an uneven sharing of the uterus so that one foal gets

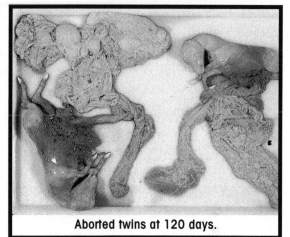

Aborted twins at 120 days.

more than half, the foal receiving less will be at an extreme disadvantage. Nutrient demand by the developing foal is greatest during the end of the second and throughout the third trimesters of pregnancy (i.e., the last three to four months). At this time, the twin which has the least amount of surface area for placental exchange starves.

The death of one of the foals frequently causes the death of the remaining foal and the pregnancy is aborted. Occasionally there is an extreme discrepancy in the amount of uterine surface area each foal has so that one foal is limited to perhaps the tip of a uterine horn. In this scenario, the limited foal might die much sooner without compromising its luckier twin, and the pregnancy is maintained as a single-ton with the dead twin being completely or partially re-sorbed. In the latter case, the dead fetus will be delivered as a mummified remnant at the time of foaling.

There seems to be a breed predilection for the occurrence of twins (Thoroughbreds, Standardbreds, and Draft mares in particular), and twins seem rarely to occur in ponies. However, I have observed twin pregnancies in a wide variety of breeds. Equine twins are fraternal twins (there has been only one reported case of identical equine twins, and that was not verified by DNA testing). Therefore, multiple equine embryos result from a double (sometimes triple) ovulation during a single estrus (heat) period. Both follicles usually ovulate roughly simultaneously or within 24 to 48 hours of each other.

The incidence of double ovulations seems to be a little higher late in the breeding season, and also seems to be more common in older mares and barren mares (as compared to younger mares and foaling mares, respectively). Individual mares which double ovulate once tend to repeat this pattern. It is recommended to breed all cycles regardless of whether there is the potential for a double ovulation, then manage the twin pregnancy to ensure reduction to a singleton. It is not uncommon for double ovulations to go undetected initially. The average longevity of a fertile stallion's semen in the mare's tract also makes it highly likely that if both ovulations occur within 72 hours of a given single breeding that the mare will conceive twins. Therefore, it is important that a mare be checked via ultrasound before 30 days gestation at least once to detect the possible presence of twins and manage them so as to ensure one has been eliminated before the endometrial cups have formed.

It is possible for an experienced veterinarian to maneuver the embryos manually via rectal palpation (with the aid of ul-trasound) so that one embryo can be guided to the tip of a uterine horn and manually crushed while leaving the second embryo undisturbed. This is most easily accomplished when the two embryos are occupying different horns. Ideally, the smaller of the two embryos is chosen as the reduction candidate. However, it is important that the embryo be "pinched off" with minimal handling of the uterus, so whichever embryo is positioned to most easily accomplish this should be pinched.

Sometimes, however, the embryos are adjacent to one another and it is not possible to separate them without risking damaging them both. In this situation, some experienced practitioners can manipulate the embryos as a unit and crush only one of them, but this is risky. Where practical, if the mare is left alone, then re-examined within a few hours, the two embryos will have moved apart and one can then be easily maneuvered and crushed. Follow-up examinations are recommended within 48 hours of "pinching off a twin" to confirm that the remaining embryo is continuing to grow and thrive, and that the pregnancy is indeed only a singleton.

It is also important to note at this point that if a mare has endometrial cysts, it is vital that a cyst not be mistaken for a twin embryo and the real single embryo be crushed by mistake. It is useful to have "mapped out" a mare's cysts (numbers, sizes, and locations) with ultrasound before breeding so the veterinarian can refer to this information. Once the embryos have become fixed in the horns, it is no longer possible to reposition them. If the embryos have settled in separate horns, one can still be manually crushed, but the older the embryos become the more difficult it is to crush them.

When twins fix together side by side in the base of the same horn (unilateral twins), the veterinarian cannot eliminate one manually without damaging the other. The good news about unilateral twins is that 80% of them self reduce to a singleton pregnancy by day 30 or so once fixation has occurred, especially if one embryonic vesicle is larger than the other. If this does not happen, a decision needs to be made before the 33rd day of gestation on how best to proceed.

Once the endometrial cups have formed, the mare likely will not begin to cycle again until sometime after what would have been 90 days of gestation, even if the whole pregnancy is lost before that time. Therefore, if the owner wants to breed the mare again that year, it is better to abort a persis-

It is rare for both twins to survive.

tent twin pregnancy with prostaglandin by the 33rd day and try again on another cycle. If the mare will not be bred again that season, the decision can be made to watch and wait a little longer to see if the pregnancy still won't self reduce. In general, however, the longer the twin embryos remain, the less likely self reduction is to occur, and after 40 days a twin pregnancy will most likely go on to abort.

There are two remaining veterinary options for reduction of the twin pregnancy. The first is a transvaginal approach using transvaginal ultrasound and rectal palpation simultaneously to place a sterile needle into one of the developing fetuses and aspirate the fluid from around it and thereby kill it. This procedure can be performed between 40 to 50 days by an experienced veterinarian using specialized equipment. Success rates are about 50%. The second option is to use a transabdominal ultrasound and aseptic technique to image one fetal heart across the mare's abdominal wall and then guide a sterile needle into the fetal heart and inject it with potassium chloride to kill the fetus, leaving the remaining twin alive. This procedure usually is most successful when performed around 120 days gestation, and again the success rate is about 50%. This latter procedure is best performed by an experienced veterinary ultrasonographer in a hospital setting.

CHAPTER 3

Gestation Length

The equine gestation length averages 340 days based on a given ovulation date. However, normal length can range from 325 days to 355-plus days. Mares which foal early in the year (i.e., January, February, and March in the Northern Hemisphere) tend to have longer gestations than mares which are foaling later (i.e., April, May, or June). Consequently, many mares do not foal right on their "due dates." Annual foaling records will help identify a more accurate date for a given mare as mares tend to repeat their previous gestation lengths, especially if they have been bred to the same stallion and are foaling around the same time each year.

Gestational length can vary in mares.

A recent study also suggests that gestation length might be somewhat correlated with individual sires as well, and it appears that colts tend to have longer gestations (one to two days) than fillies. The bottom line: Watch the mare for signs of approaching foaling as she often chooses to ignore the calendar.

Foalings that occur outside the accepted normal range result in foals that are premature, postmature/dysmature, or result in abortions, depending on when the delivery occurred. Foals born between 300 to 325 days of gestation are considered premature and require intensive nursing and medical care to survive. The earlier the foal is born relative to its expected due date, the less well equipped it is to handle life outside the womb. Fetuses delivered before 300 days of gestation are considered abortions and, if not dead at delivery, die soon afterward despite human assistance.

AT A GLANCE

• The average gestation length is 340 days.

• Foals born after 355 days or more are considered "overdue."

• Inducing parturition before a mare is outwardly ready will likely result in a foal which cannot handle life outside the womb.

• Infected fescue grass can cause a number of problems for pregnant mares.

On the other end of the spectrum are those foals considered "overdue," born after 355 days or more. Many mares have carried for a year or longer and still delivered apparently normal foals. In general, however, "overdue" foals tend to be smaller rather than larger than normal-term foals, and they tend to be thin. Often, too, they will resemble premature foals in that they are down in their fetlocks and pasterns, have silky hair coats, and other signs of prematurity. Such foals are labeled postmature or dysmature. In these pregnancies, it is thought that the rate of nutrient exchange to the foal across the placenta might be decreased, which slows the development of the foal and results in a prolonged gestation. This condition is more commonly observed in older mares which have foaled before and could be caused by age changes and "wear and tear" in the endometrium. In these cases, it is always best to allow the mare to continue her gestation until she is ready to foal.

Inducing labor poses a danger when an "overdue" mare shows no other signs that she is close to foaling — udder development, relaxation of the ligaments around the tailhead, etc. Inducement can result in a foal that is not ready to be born and is in fact premature despite what the calendar says. The exception to this "overdue" scenario is the mare which is experiencing a prolonged gestation due to fescue toxicity.

Tall fescue (*festuca arundinaceae*) is a common pasture grass of the Southeastern and Northwestern United States. Its hardy nature and ease of growth make it a popular forage and an acceptable source of nutrition for horses. Trouble arises when the grass is infected with a fungal endophyte, *Acremonium coenophialum*.

This endophyte lives in a symbiotic relationship with the grass and is the source of toxins associated with causing prolonged gestation (13 to 14 months), dystocia, neonatal morbidity and mortality, agalactia (absence of milk), and retained placenta in mares consuming infected fescue during late gestation. Diagnosis is usually based primarily on the signs of poor udder development and prolonged gestation in pregnant mares known to have ingested infected fescue.

Pastures should be tested each fall before the breeding

Test pastures for the presence of fescue.

season to determine whether they are endophyte-infected and to what extent. The best way to manage this problem is to avoid it by removing mares from infected pastures and not feeding hay made from infected fields after day 300 of the gestation. In addition, pastures should be managed to minimize the amount of endophyte. Reseeding with endophyte-free seed, mowing frequently to prevent formation of seed heads, and overseeding infected pastures with a legume are beneficial. Late-term mares which have been exposed to the fescue endophyte toxins should be monitored for failure of normal mammary development.

To treat or prevent agalactia, the attending veterinary might recommend administering a prolactin stimulating agent (reserpine, domperidone, or acepromazine). Foalings should be attended closely because dystocias are common. Foals are often oversized and weak and frequently they are malpositioned for delivery. The mare's pelvic ligaments frequently are not relaxed, which often makes delivery more difficult. These foals require good nursing care and medical treatment to survive, and the foaling must be managed to safeguard the mare's future fertility. Fescue mares often retain their placentas, which tend to be thick with edema.

CHAPTER 4

General Broodmare Management

The pregnant mare, like all horses, thrives on routine. Changes in the mare's housing, diet, companions, exercise, and handling should be avoided or made gradually when possible. Chronic medical conditions should be addressed, as should routine upkeep of feet, deworming, etc. Ideally, any procedures that might be extra stressful to the mare (such as teeth floating) should be performed before the mare is bred so that it does not become an issue during the pregnancy, and all vaccinations should be up to date at least two weeks before the first breeding if possible. Pregnant mares which are stressed by vanning should stay home, and all pregnant mares should not be hauled for long periods or over great distances if at all possible. If a long trip home from a breeding facility is necessary, it should be done when the pregnancy is well established and stress should be kept to a minimum.

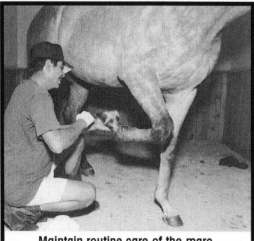

Maintain routine care of the mare.

Pregnant mares ideally

are housed at pasture in small, compatible groups, and have separate stabling from "transitory" horse populations. They should be kept in seclusion. All new horses brought to any farm should be isolated for a minimum of three weeks and closely monitored for any signs of illness before coming into contact with the resident population. This is particularly important on farms that house pregnant mares.

Pastures should be well maintained and safely fenced, and barns should be well ventilated and comfortably bedded with clean shavings, paper, or straw. Large box stalls (14x14 minimum) are ideal so that the mares can move around and lie down and get up easily.

> ## AT A GLANCE
>
> • Don't make abrupt changes to a pregnant mare's routine.
>
> • Pregnant mares need adequate exercise.
>
> • Mares should be up to date on vaccines, dewormed prior to being bred, then maintained on a regular deworming schedule after 60 days of gestation.
>
> • Weigh pregnant mares every one to two months to assess their weight gain.
>
> • A mare's nutrient requirements increase during the last three to four months of gestation.

A pregnant mare needs adequate exercise on a daily basis. Ideally this means turnout into a good-sized paddock or pasture. Mares which are able to stay in work and conceive at the time of breeding can continue at their previous level of conditioning provided they do not become overly sweaty or tired. Now is not the time to begin training her for an event course or prolonged park class. Opt instead for a leisurely trail ride. Strenuous exercise and jumping should be curtailed from the start of the pregnancy, and riding probably should be discontinued by the time the mare is beginning to show outwardly (i.e., halfway into the second trimester).

Open and maiden mares should receive all their annual vaccinations before foaling. These include eastern-western encephalomyelitis, tetanus toxoid, herpesvirus types I and IV (rhino), influenza (flu), and Potomac horse fever and rabies in endemic areas. Strangles vaccine also may be given prior to breeding if the mare is at risk of exposure. In general, no vaccinations should be given during the first 90 days of gestation (the period during which the mare's immune system is adjusting to the pregnancy and the foal's vital organs are forming). Pregnant mares should be vaccinated against rhino/herpes viral abortion at three, five, seven, and nine months of gestation. In endemic areas, botulism toxoid also should be administered to previously unvaccinated mares at eight, nine, and 10 months of gestation, and at one month prior to foaling in previously vaccinated mares. The protocol for botulism toxoid is designed to boost the level of antibodies against botulism in the mare's first milk (colostrum) to provide her foal with immunity against botulism (shaker foal disease).

In general, with the exception of rhino and botulism, all other vaccinations in pregnant mares should be avoided until one month prior to foaling. Late-term mares receive their annual boosters of eastern-western encephalomyelitis, tetanus, flu and rabies (where endemic) one month before foaling, again to boost the foal's colostral immunity.

Control of parasitic infections in pregnant mares is extremely important. She should not have to compete with intestinal worms for the nutrients she eats, and the damage caused to the mare's intestinal lining and blood vessels by migrating larvae is debilitating to her and potentially life-threatening. Parasite control will differ from farm to farm as factors such as pasture stocking rates, climate, and degree of parasite infestation will differ. However, most parasite control plans will combine the use of anthelmintics ("dewormers"), pasture management, stocking rates, and routine fecal monitoring.

Under a veterinarian's direction, rotational treatment of pregnant mares with the three classes of anthelmintics (Avermectins {Ivermectin}, Benzimidazoles {Fenbendazole, Febantel, etc.}, and Pyrimidines {Pyrantel Pamoate and Tartarate} can be performed using varying schedules tailored to best meet the requirements of the season and given farm situation. Mares should be dewormed before being bred, and administration of anthelmintics to pregnant mares probably should be avoided for the first 60 days of gestation. All horses on a given farm should be dewormed along with the broodmares.

Organophosphate wormers and combination products containing organophosphates should be avoided in pregnant mares. Ideally, pasture stocking rates are kept low (i.e., a minimum of one to five acres of pasture per horse if possible) as "di-

Parasite control is important.

lution is the solution" to pasture parasitic infestation rates. Parasitic larva and eggs are passed in an infected horse's feces. The pasture becomes increasingly infested with infectious stage larva as buildup of the manure increases. The fewer horses on a given piece of land, the less manure produced. Likewise, the less manure left on a pasture, the fewer parasitic larva with which the grazing or feeding horse can reinfest itself. Rotating, chain harrowing, and mowing pastures and picking up manure help decrease exposure.

Individual fecal samples on all horses are important as some individuals seem to be more susceptible to increased parasitic loads than others. Lactating mares for instance often appear to be infected more easily with intestinal parasites than non-lactating mares. These "weak sisters" serve as a chronic source of reinfection for the other horses, and could require different anthelmintic schedules and frequency. As always, pregnant mares should be medicated as little as possible. Effective parasite management for the entire farm and individually tailored anthelmintic treatment schedules help maintain the pregnant mare in premium condition while minimizing her drug exposure.

FEEDING

Following appropriate guidelines to ensure that a mare is achieving a properly balanced diet is the obvious goal of any nutrition program, but make adjustments as needed to maintain pregnant mares at an optimal body condition. Mares which are too thin at foaling will not milk well. Mares which

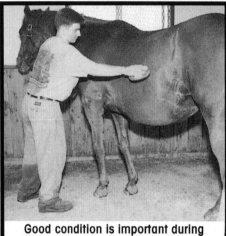

Good condition is important during pregnancy.

are too fat are susceptible to developing laminitis and metabolic disorders, especially during late pregnancy or after foaling.

The optimally conditioned mare should have a shiny coat and bright eye, and you should be able to "just" feel her ribs and not have to dig for them or be able to see them from five steps back. Her back, loin, and croup areas should appear rounded and smooth with muscling. The

back, pelvic, and tail head bones should not feel or look prominent, and her neck should not be thin and "ewe" shaped from lack of condition. At the same time she should not have rolls of fat over her back and withers, her crest should not be rock solid and ready to fall over, and there should not be pads of fat around the root of her tail.

Once you have established that your mare looks optimal, weigh her (or tape her), and record her weight. "Eyeballing" any animal can be misleading, because changes might be subtle from day to day. Pregnant mares should be weighed every one to two months to accurately assess their progress. For a 1,000- to 1,200-pound mare to maintain her optimal pre-pregnancy condition, she should gain somewhere between 150 to 200 pounds during the last trimester to allow for the weight of the foal, the fetal membranes, and fluids. (The average birth weight of a healthy foal is approximately 9% to 10% of the mare's body weight.) Remember the foal's greatest nutrient needs and weight gains occur during the last three to four months of gestation. Correspondingly, that is also when the mare's nutrient requirements increase above maintenance levels and she needs to be fed a more nutrient rich ration.

Feeding any animal is a matter of supplying energy, protein, vitamins, minerals, and (in the case of herbivores) roughage in the correct amounts to meet the metabolic needs of the animal and keep the digestive tract functioning smoothly.

A pregnant mare's energy and protein requirements are at maintenance levels during the first eight months of gestation provided she was in the proper body condition at the start of her pregnancy. During the ninth, 10th, and 11th months of gestation the Digestible Energy Requirements of the mare increase to 1.11, 1.13, and 1.20 times the maintenance requirement, respectively. Non-pregnant mares require a total ration that is 7% to 8% protein on a 90% dry matter basis. Pregnant mares require 9% to 10% protein of the total ration, and early and late lactating mares require 12% and 10% total dietary protein respectively. Grains are more protein and energy dense than grass hay. As nutrient demands increase, the amount of grain in the total ration also should increase. Likewise, as pregnancy advances, the mare's gastrointestinal tract competes with the growing foal for available space in the mare's abdomen, and she is inclined to consume less hay.

Horses require a diet that is largely made up of forages to keep their digestive system functioning properly. Concentrates (grain mixtures with added vitamins and minerals) complement the nutrient content of the forage portion of the ration. At maintenance requirements, mares in general will eat about two pounds of grass hay per 100 pounds of body weight per day, and late gestation mares will eat one to two pounds of hay per 100 pounds of body weight and about one pound of grain per 100 pounds of body weight per day. Grain meals should be divided over the day so no more than 5 pounds are provided at any single meal. Assuming a grass hay protein content around 8%, a pregnant mare needs a grain ration that is about 14% protein to round out the overall protein content of her diet to meet her 10% need.

The nutrient content of grass pasture changes from season to season, and the quality of hay changes depending on the phase of plant growth when it was cut, the weather conditions when it lay drying on the fields, and the quality of the field from which it was cut. The nutrient content and quality of all forages needs to be analyzed routinely throughout the year. Without knowing the quality of the forages being fed, it is impossible to know what mixture of grain, vitamins, and minerals is required to properly complement the forage. Most commercially available feeds are formulated to be balanced and complete, but again this is based on suppositions on the quality of the forages that will be fed. Every horse manager should have forages routinely analyzed two to four times annually, and make adjustments to the concentrate rations accordingly, in order to complement the forages properly. Properly balancing a ration is best done with the advice of an equine nutritionist. Many veterinary or agricultural colleges have nutritionists who can act as consultants to individual mare owners, or county extension agents can offer referral services to qualified equine nutritionists.

Lastly, mares should be able to take full advantage of the feed that is offered to them. Mares' dental needs should be attended to regularly, and they should have their teeth floated before breeding so they are not stressed by the procedure while pregnant. Mares should not have to compete with stronger, greedier pasture mates for their meals. Proper bunk space and spacing of feed should be provided so all mares housed in a group situation can eat their full ration in peace.

Where the management system permits, bring mares in at

mealtimes and feed their concentrate rations individually in stalls along with their hay. Hay and/or grass, clean water, and mineral salt blocks should be available to mares at all times. Mares turned out onto lush green pastures for the first time should be introduced to these pastures slowly so as not to disrupt their normal gut function. Mares should be fed a hay ration before turnout so they are not ravenous when they reach the grass, and it is nice to have hay available in racks in the pasture as well so the mares can have a choice.

CHAPTER 5
High Risk Pregnancies

Supplementing the pregnant mare with progesterone is sometimes controversial. Therapy can be overused and is not always necessary in every mare which receives oral altrenogest (Regumate™) or injectable progesterone in oil. However, in specific situations, supplementing a pregnant mare with progesterone is necessary to maintain the pregnancy. There also are some infertile mares which maintain accepted, normal progesterone levels, but seem to be better able to establish and maintain a pregnancy is they receive additional progesterone supplementation..

Circulating progesterone is necessary for the mare to maintain and support a pregnancy. The minimal level of progesterone required appears to be 2 nanograms per milliliter (ng/ml). Reference values will differ from laboratory to laboratory, but at the New York State Diagnostic Laboratory at Cornell University Veterinary College, the accepted normal range for an early pregnant or mid- to late-diestrous mare is 5 ng/ml or above. After ovulation, it takes the corpus luteum (CL) on the ovary four to six days to mature and produce progesterone at this level. In the pregnant mare, this primary CL will continue to produce this hormone for the first 120 days of gestation. Once the endometrial cups are formed and begin producing equine chorionic gonadotropin, secondary

CLs form on the ovaries as a backup to ensure that the ovaries will produce adequate levels of progesterone until the placenta is producing adequate levels of progestogens.

The placenta begins producing progestogens between days 50 and 70 of gestation. During the second half of the pregnancy, placental progestogens are responsible for pregnancy maintenance. The assays available for measuring progesterone in the mare usually do not measure the placental progestogens but only the ovarian progesterone.

> ## AT A GLANCE
>
> • Progesterone therapy can help an injured or ill mare maintain her pregnancy.
>
> • Progesterone should be given under a veterinarian's direction.
>
> • Mares abort for a number of reasons, including illness, injury, and placentitis.
>
> • A mare which aborts should be isolated and monitored by a vet.

Therefore, it is normal to measure progesterone levels in a mare after 150 or so days of gestation and find them numerically low even though the placental "progesterone" is maintaining the pregnancy just fine.

Any cause of decreased production of ovarian progesterone during the first 100-plus days of the pregnancy endangers the pregnancy. Primary failure of the corpus luteum to produce adequate progesterone levels is rare. Progesterone production is not constant over a 24-hour period, so measured levels at any given moment might be low even though overall production is fine. It might be necessary to sample a mare twice during a 24-hour period to get an accurate picture.

If the ovary is exposed to prostaglandin during the first 100-plus days of gestation and progesterone production is decreased or terminated, the pregnancy is in danger of being lost. Inflammation of the endometrium (endometritis, usually due to infection) or failure of maternal recognition of pregnancy will result in prostaglandin being produced and destruction of the CL(s). The most common reason for luteal (and embryonic) failure before day 20 is a chronically infected uterus. Progesterone has been shown to inhibit the action of white blood cells within the uterus to clean up infection. Progesterone also stimulates the uterus to produce glandular secretions and histotroph to help support any possible pregnancy. These fluids provide a wonderful medium for bacteria or fungal organisms to set up residence. For these two reasons, it is not advisable to give a mare exogenous progesterone if a uterine infection is suspected, as progesterone has the potential to make the infection worse and damage the endometrium. In a worst case scenario, mares with undetected infections which are placed on supplemental progesterone then not closely monitored can develop a pyometra (uterus that is filled with fluid and pus) as the additional progesterone keeps the cervix closed and might not permit the infection to drain. Pyometra causes severe damage to the mare's uterine lining.

Mares which have free fluid in their uterus on ultrasound examination during the diestrous period or vulvar discharge are suspect for having an infection. Infected mares also could have uterine edema on ultrasound, and their tract could be palpably heavy and/or thickened. A uterine infection is not always readily apparent, however, and any mare placed on progesterone therapy needs to be watched closely just in case her uterus "blows" with an obvious infection.

Mares which lose pregnancies due to a failure of maternal recognition require supplementation before or by the 14th day after ovulation. Mares which are suspect for this condition likely will benefit from supplementation if it is initiated very early (i.e., about four days after ovulation). It is important to examine these mares closely during the post-breeding period to ensure they have no signs of lingering inflammation before treatment starts. In my experience, early supplementation also seems to help some mares which have no discernible reason for not being pregnant after two to three cycles of breeding. Many of these mares fail to show a discernible embryo the 12th day after ovulation and breeding, and often they retain their CLs. The mares have clean uterine cytologies when examined during the beginning of the next estrus. The semen being used appears to be of good quality or the stallion is impregnating other mares, but this particular mare is still not pregnant. Some of these mares seem to benefit from early progesterone supplementation and successfully go on to carry a pregnancy after it is instituted, although the reason why is not clear.

A normal pregnant mare which becomes injured or ill is also at risk of losing her pregnancy. Progesterone supplementation could help her maintain the pregnancy until she is recovered and able once again to support the developing foal herself. Any condition that releases endotoxins into the mare's circulation (a strangulating intestinal colic or diarrhea, for example) will induce prostaglandin release. While the pregnancy depends on the ovarian CLs, subsequent pregnancy loss is due to the loss of ovarian progesterone. Later on during gestation, it is thought that perhaps prolonged exposure of the uterus to high levels of endotoxin-induced prostaglandin results in contractions and subsequent abortion of the fetus. Supplementing endotoxic mares with exogenous progesterone has been proven effective in preventing pregnancy loss in many affected individuals. Initiate progesterone therapy as soon as possible once the insult to the mare's system has begun. Fetal viability needs to be monitored (usually by checking for a fetal heartbeat with ultrasound). Affected mares at less than 120 to 150 days of gestation will need supplementation at least until placental maintenance of the pregnancy begins (i.e., day 120 to 150) because once the CLs have been destroyed they do not come back. Progesterone therapy in later gestation mares with well-established placentas can be discontinued at the discretion of an attending veterinarian once the mare has fully recovered from her illness.

The role stress plays in causing sick or injured mares to

abort is unclear. Levels of adrenal corticosteroids rise during times of stress, but in practice very high levels given repeatedly over several days are required to cause a mare to abort or go into labor. It has also been proposed that periods of stress could suppress progesterone production, although experiments have not shown this. Without a doubt, however, some stressed mares do seem prone to pregnancy loss. Therefore, any injury or illness is cause for concern and veterinary advice should be sought.

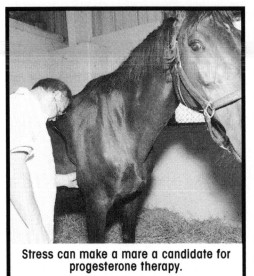

Stress can make a mare a candidate for progesterone therapy.

Options for supplementary progesterone therapy are limited. Injectable progesterone in oil is given daily in the mare's muscle and is the only proven available alternative that is safe and adequately maintains blood progesterone levels when the mare is unable or fiercely unwilling to accept oral supplementation. Altrenogest is a synthetic progesterone (Regumate™) that is given orally on a daily basis. It can be administered by dose syringe or put in the feed if the mare is being fed individually and will lick up all of her grain ration. Altrenogest should be handled with care because it can be absorbed across a person's skin. The person handling and administering the drug should wear gloves and wash thoroughly afterward. Both forms of progesterone should be administered at the direction of a supervising veterinarian.

Once supplementation begins, the next question for the veterinarian is when is it safe to discontinue treatment? The whole purpose of initiating therapy is to provide added or replacement support of ovarian, luteal progesterone. Therefore, supplementation should not be discontinued prior to 120 to 150 days of gestation. In general, once the placenta is producing adequate levels of progestogens and its uterine attachments have matured, an ovarian source of progesterone is no longer needed. This occurs sometime between 100 and 150 days of gestation. If the pregnancy is progressing normally, I like to wean mares off supplementation beginning around day 120 so it is discontinued by day 150. This is done by decreasing the oral dose by half and giving daily for seven days, then decreasing the frequency of the half dose to every other day for seven to 10 days. While it has been shown that treatment can be stopped "cold turkey," it is less of a shock to the mare's system and the pregnancy to do so gradually. The mare should be rectally palpated and an ultrasound examination (both rectally and transabdominally) performed to assess cervical and uterine tone and to check on fetal viability and placentation before weaning off supplementation. Sometimes blood progesterone levels can be checked as well. If the levels are still above 2 ng/ml (and preferably more than 5 ng/ml), the decision to discontinue therapy can be made with the feeling of a little extra security. (Progesterone assays will only reflect endogenous production of progesterone if altrenogest is being given, but do not discern between ovarian and injected progesterone so measured levels will be misleading in the latter instance.) Likewise, estrone sulfate levels can be checked to assess that the fetal-placental unit appears to be functioning normally.

Many mares are maintained on progesterone supplementation until just before term (usually discontinued by 325 days) with no adverse effects. If a doubt exists, the pregnancy is particularly valuable, or the owner is nervous, I prefer to continue therapy.

Once therapy is initiated, the uterus needs to be monitored for infection and also fetal death. While the mare is on progesterone, she will not return to estrus. Failure to detect the loss of an embryo needlessly maintains the mare in a diestrous state and is a waste of time and money because of the increased amount of time the mare spends open and the cost of the supplementation itself.

Lastly, progesterone keeps the uterus quiet and the cervix closed. Once the pregnancy reaches the fetal stage, the fetal tissues might not be resorbed fully by the uterus if the developing foal dies. Supplemental progesterone could prevent these retained tissues from being aborted. If this occurs, it is possible that the fetal remnants will become mummified as the fluid is slowly removed from them by the mare's tract. Once a mummy has formed, it might not be possible to remove it from the uterus. Should this occur, the mare's reproductive career is over. In addition, an infection could enter the occupied uterus and become established in the mummified tissues. The result would be a severe and dangerous infection.

ABORTION

Equine abortion generally refers to the premature expulsion of the fetus between the 50th and 300th day of gesta-

tion. Mares abort for any number of reasons. Abnormalities in the placenta or the endometrium also place the developing foal at risk. Late-developing or long-standing reproductive tract infections can cause inflammation and damage to the placenta, resulting in pregnancy loss. A number of infectious diseases that affect the horse also can cause abortion. Nutrition, genetic mistakes, exposure to environmental toxins, and injury can all cause abortion.

Abortion occurs in about 10% of all mares.

Abortion rates are in the neighborhood of 10% of all equine pregnancies, and unfortunately only about 50% of equine abortions receive a definitive diagnosis as to why they occurred. The placenta and the uterine lining are the developing foal's lifeline to the outside world. The connection between the two supplies oxygen and nutrition to the foal and helps remove waste products throughout the foal's uterine life. Scar tissue or fibrosis of the mare's uterine lining is formed at the expense of the uterine glands and other supportive tissues of the endometrium. Endometrial glands that are "choked off" by fibrosis are unable to produce histotroph to support the pregnancy early on, and placentas from mares which have an endometrium that is atrophied and fibrotic often show corresponding abnormalities in the development of the microvilli on the chorionic surface. Developing foals from these mares likely experience poor nutrient exchange across the uterine and placental interface. There is a higher incidence of abortion and pregnancy loss in mares with uterine pathology.

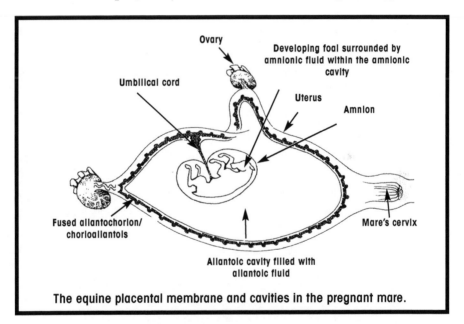

The equine placental membrane and cavities in the pregnant mare.

The equine umbilical cord is quite long compared to those in other domestic species. As a result, the equine fetus, wrapped in its amnion, is quite mobile on its "umbilical tether" within the allantoic cavity for a long period during early to mid gestation. Excessively long umbilical cords can be prone to torsion if the fetus somersaults excessively, and abortion due to strangulation of the blood supply within the umbilical cord is sometimes recognized in aborted equine fetuses. However, the umbilical cord of horses often contains many twists without compromising the fetus, and this condition should only be suspected if bruising, clotting, or rupture of the aborted fetus' cord is seen in addition to twisting.

Placentitis is an inflammation of the placenta. Usually it is caused by an infection on the surface of the placenta. It is thought that infecting organisms come from long-standing uterine infections, or gain access to the placental surface via a bacteremia in the mare's bloodstream. The most common scenario is a placentitis caused by an ascending infection through the mare's cervix. Any condition that compromises the integrity of the cervical barrier predisposes a mare to developing a placentitis and subsequently aborting. Cervical trauma (lacerations) at foaling that is severe can result in scar formation or deficits in the cervix that prevent the mare from forming a tight closure of the cervix during diestrus and pregnancy. Chronic irritation and bacterial contamination caused by pneumovagina, urine pooling, or small recto-vaginal fistulas can cause the cervix to become inflamed and open, allowing the bacterial or fungal organisms access to the uterine environment. A variety of organisms have been isolated from placentitis cases with the majority of them (such as *Streptococcus* species, *Escherichia coli*, and *Staphylococcus* species) being opportunists that were in the right place at the right time to cause a problem.

Most cases occur during the last 60 days of gestation. Outwardly the mares typically demonstrate signs of premature mammary development and a vaginal discharge that can range from serous to hemorrhagic to frank pus. Diagnosis may be made by simple speculum examination, which might show an inflamed cervix discharging an exudate through the external cervical os. If the vaginal discharge is bloody, a speculum examination will help distinguish a placentitis case from a case of vaginal varicose veins.

(Bleeding from vaginal varicose veins is sometimes seen in mares during pregnancy and occasionally during estrus and is most likely due to the increase in blood circulation and pressure seen in the vaginal region. Unless the bleeding is excessive and the mare is becoming anemic, usually no attempt is made to ligate or cauterize the offending vessel, and the mare is simply kept quiet and under close observation. Frequently she will also have a Caslick's procedure to decrease the likelihood of any further vaginal irritation to the engorged veins. The condition usually resolves spontaneously after the mare foals, but foaling should be closely attended in case the mare ruptures a particularly large vessel.)

Placentitis also can be confirmed via rectal ultrasound, which might show placental thickening in the caudal uterine body and adjacent to the internal cervical os of the cervix. There could also be evidence of premature placental separation in this region. Treatment includes broad spectrum, systemic antimicrobials, anti-inflammatory drugs, and stall rest. Using progesterone for uterine infections is somewhat controversial. Exogenous progesterone can help quiet the uterus in placentitis cases in an attempt to maintain the pregnancy. If progesterone is used, fetal viability should be monitored closely and supplementation discontinued the moment fetal death is recognized. A veterinarian also might choose to use other uterine quieting agents such as isoxsuprine or clenbuterol (where available).

Frequently placentitis is too advanced when first noticed to save the pregnancy, but treatment occasionally succeeds and the fetus makes it to term. Foals born with affected placentas are frequently septic and weak and require intensive nursing and medical care to survive. The mare likewise should be treated aggressively for endometritis after aborting or foaling with sterile saline, uterine lavage and antibiotics or antifungals as indicated by culture and sensitivity results. Damage caused to the mare's uterus by a placentitis could hurt her future reproductive capabilities, and any predisposing anatomical conditions should be repaired before the next breeding to prevent the condition from recurring.

There are several infectious equine diseases that can cause abortion in mares. Among these diseases the most common are equine herpesvirus (type I and type IV), equine viral arteritis, Potomac horse fever, and leptospirosis. The key to managing any pregnant mare is to isolate her from any possible sources of infection, keep stress levels to a minimum, and vaccinate her appropriately. Equine herpesvirus type I typically causes respiratory disease (rhinopneumonitis) in young horses, but also can cause abortion in pregnant mares, neurologic disease occasionally in any horse, and neonatal pneumonia and mortality. Herpesvirus type IV typically only causes respiratory disease, but has been associated with abortions in mares. Clinically the abortions caused by type I and type IV are indistinguishable.

As with other herpesviruses, equine herpes virus will lie dormant within a previously infected horse and become active during periods of stress. These "silent carriers" can infect other horses, and they could shed the virus without showing any outward clinical signs. The virus gains access to its host when horses inhale it as an aerosol transmission or sniff aborted fetal materials. Infected pregnant mares could show varying degrees of respiratory signs and fever, or show no sign of illness until they abort. Abortions typically occur after seven months of gestation, and could occur anywhere from 14 to 120 days after exposure to the virus.

In the past, it was common for an "abortion storm" to go through a farm. Today, the incidence of mass abortions has decreased because horsemen have become better at managing their mares to decrease their exposure, and vaccination of pregnant mares has become widespread. However, no vaccine is 100% effective in preventing disease, and some mares will not mount a good response to vaccination and remain susceptible if exposed. Typically these days "Rhino abortions" occur sporadically but are still responsible for a large percentage of the equine abortions diagnosed. Pregnant mares should be kept apart from all young horse and transient horse populations (i.e., weanlings, yearlings, show and racehorses, and sales horses). Any and all aborted membranes, fetal fluids, and tissues should be removed promptly, and contaminated bedding should be removed and stalls disinfected in such a way that there is no chance of other horses being exposed to the virus (i.e., do not spread contaminated bedding on pastures and do not leave aborted materials in a bucket or wheelbarrow).

Mares should be vaccinated at a minimum at five, seven, and nine months of gestation. Immune response to herpes viral antigens are short-lived, so vaccinations must be repeated regularly for an animal to maintain a good level of immunity. Some veterinarians even recommend vaccinating mares starting at three months of gestation when exposure is likely. All other horses on the premises should be vaccinated regularly for "Rhino" as well to decrease the likelihood of an outbreak.

Equine viral arteritis abortions have been observed sporadically, and positive titers confirming exposure to the virus are more common in Standardbreds than in any other breed. EVA causes widespread vascular necrosis in affected individuals, resulting in fever, depression, swelling of the limbs, and sometimes the face and abdomen, conjunctivitis, temporary infertility in bred mares, and abortion in pregnant mares anywhere from three to eight weeks after exposure to the virus. Airborne transmission can result in outbreaks, and the virus also is transmitted venereally to mares from infected, shedder stallions. (The virus resides in the accessory sex glands of the stallion and can be shed in the semen in some individuals.). A note of caution to breeders: This virus will freeze readily and contaminate frozen and shipped semen as well as fresh.

Vaccination efforts are aimed primarily at the stallions. Stallions should be checked for negative titers and vaccinated around four weeks before the start of the breeding season. Stallions which have positive titers and were not previously vaccinated should be tested to see if they are shedding the virus in their semen (shedding can occur for years after initial clinical disease affected the stallion). Stallions which are confirmed to be shedding virus should only be bred to mares which have a positive titer against the disease (either through previous natural exposure or by vaccination at least three weeks before breeding). Mares bred to shedder stallions should be isolated from other in-foal mares and sero-negative mares for a minimum of three weeks just in case these recently bred mares do manifest clinical disease and shed the virus despite precautions. Vaccination of pregnant mares with the modified live vaccine is not recommended. Depending on the horse's export status, preventive vaccination may not be pursued because of export regulations barring sero-positive horses and/or their semen from entering certain countries. With the increased popularity of using frozen semen in certain breeds, it might become prudent to vaccinate mares without positive titers before breeding with frozen semen if the stallion's status is unknown.

Potomac horse fever is caused by the Ehrlichial organism, *Ehrlichia risticii,* and is thought to be transmitted by some form of biting insect, although the exact vector is unknown. An increased incidence of this disease is usually seen in endemic locations during the late spring through the early fall months, but cases are sporadic and not thought to be spread from horse to horse. Potomac horse fever can cause severe diarrhea, fever, laminitis, and sometimes death, and it has been associated with causing abortions in mares. Mares experimentally infected with the organism typically aborted two months later. Mild and subclinical forms of the fever occur commonly, and it is conceivable that a mare might abort suddenly with no previously recognized illness. When clinical signs are present, veterinary treatment of the mare with oxytetracycline during the acute colitis might reduce the incidence of subsequent abortion. A vaccine against Potomac horse fever is available, but its effectiveness in preventing abortion is unknown. In endemic areas, it might be prudent to vaccinate broodmares before breeding.

The incidence of recognized equine abortions caused by leptospirosis has increased in recent years. There are different bacterial strains, or serovars, of the *Leptospira* organism that have been reported to cause equine abortion, but the most common one is *Leptospira pomona*. The source of the organism is any infected animal. White-tailed deer are thought to serve as a reservoir for *Leptospira* in the Northeast. Horses are typically exposed when their mucous membranes or cut or abraded skin come into contact with the organism that has been shed, usually in the urine of an infected animal. Signs of urinary tract infection are seen, and some animals experience kidney failure. Other clinical manifestations of leptospirosis in horses include fever, jaundice (liver disease, hemolytic anemia), chronic uveitis (moon blindness or periodic ophthalmia), and abortion. Signs can be mild or severe, and abortion usually follows clinical illness by two weeks.

Mares which experience leptospiral abortions usually have very high titers to the offending organism in their bloodstream, and the organism can be isolated from their urine for as long as three months following the initial infection. Shedding mares need to be isolated from other horses, and all contaminated bedding, discharges, and aborted materials must be disposed of carefully and all contacting surfaces disinfected to ensure that the organism is not spread to another animal. A note of caution: Humans are susceptible to leptospiral infections as well, and extreme caution and sanitation should be employed when handling contaminated materials. Affected mares can be treated with penicillin, streptomycin, or oxytetracycline by a veterinarian, and treatment could decrease the shedder period and prevent infection of the fetus and subsequent abortion. There is no approved leptospirosis vaccine for horses. The best method of prevention is to eliminate exposure. This is best accomplished by keeping horses fenced away from wet areas and areas of runoff from other animals.

WHAT TO DO WHEN MARES ABORT

What should the mare's caretakers do in the event of an equine abortion? Many abortions occur unnoticed until a routine veterinary examination shows the mare to be open or her abdomen fails to enlarge as expected and the veterinarian confirms the owner's suspicions. Most commonly these mares were out at pasture and not closely observed. Mares which are monitored closely, however, are unlikely to abort without someone noticing, even if it is to only notice some discharge or blood on the mare's tail when she is led in from pasture.

All aborted materials should be saved in a plastic bag that will not leak and kept cool until a veterinarian can examine and sample them. Or they should be placed in a cooler with

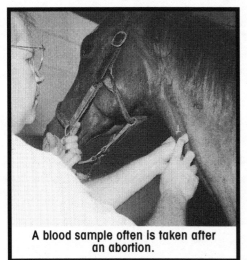

A blood sample often is taken after an abortion.

ice and taken to the nearest diagnostic lab. Gloves should be worn when handling all aborted tissues, and the person should wash up thoroughly afterwards. Pregnant women, children, and immune-compromised individuals should not handle the aborted remains or discharging fluids. Any bedding should be carefully removed and disposed of and the ground surface on which the aborted remains lay should be disinfected.

The mare should be isolated immediately in a comfortable stall and closely monitored until the veterinarian can arrive. The veterinarian will give the mare a thorough physical examination, take blood and urine samples, and perform a culture and cytology of her uterus. The mare's reproductive tract will be assessed via rectal palpation and ultrasound and vaginal speculum and digital examinations for signs of infection or injury. Next, the veterinarian will carefully examine

the aborted fetal remains to estimate fetal age and development and the degree of decomposition. The veterinarian also
will examine the placenta for abnormalities, and to make sure
none of the placental membranes has been retained.
Treatment will be initiated (antibiotics, anti-inflammatories,
uterine lavage, etc.) depending on the exam findings. The
veterinarian either will submit the entire fetal tissues on ice
to a diagnostic laboratory, or gather samples of the fetal
heart, lungs, spleen, kidneys, liver, heart, blood, and stomach
contents along with placental samples. The fixed tissues will
be sectioned and examined microscopically for pathologic
changes, and the fresh tissues will be cultured or otherwise
processed in the laboratory to perform bacterial and viral iso-
lations. Tissues not submitted for analysis should be burned
or buried well away from any other horses.

The veterinarian might take blood samples from the mare's
stable or pasture mates. The veterinarian also might perform
follow-up examinations and a uterine biopsy, and take follow-
up blood samples from the mare and her sampled pasture
and barn mates. A thorough history also is important to
solving the diagnostic dilemma that many abortions pose,
and complete records on the mare and histories concerning
any recent illnesses or arrivals on the farm should be made
known and available to the examining veterinarian. It is important that the mare who aborted be kept isolated from her
(pregnant) horse companions until the veterinarian indicates
that the risk of the mare shedding offending organisms has
passed. It pays to be vigilant and cautious.

Any pregnant mares who are injured, colicking, or showing
signs of depression, fever, decreased appetite, vaginal discharge, premature mammary development, or any other abnormal sign should be examined by a veterinarian as soon as
possible. Early detection and treatment of sick mares might
save pregnancies in some cases.

CHAPTER 6

Pre-Foaling Management

A mare should be brought inside at night beginning 45 to 30 days before her due date. This is done for two reasons. The first is so she can become comfortable with the surroundings and feel that the foaling stall is a safe, private place. Mares who are not at ease might delay foaling and prolong their labor until they feel more secure. Such a delay can lead to complications.

The second reason is to introduce the mare to all the local pathogens, giving her time to build immunity and concentrate this immunity in her first milk, or colostrum. The foal receives all its immunity for the first three or so months of its

life via the antibodies absorbed from the mare's colostrum during the first 24 hours of life. By introducing the mare to the local organisms ahead of time, you are, in effect, protecting the foal.

The foaling stall should be a minimum of 14 x 14, have solid walls that rise at least three feet from the

The foaling stall should be at least 14 x 14.

floor, be free of any sharp edges, and be well ventilated but draft-free. The stall should be kept clean, dry, and well bedded at all times. The mare should be isolated from transient horses (show and sale horses) and young horses (weanlings and yearlings) to avoid exposing her or her unborn foal to any new and/or particularly virulent pathogen (rhinopneumonitis in particular). Ideally, foaling mares live in a separate barn and get turned out during the day in small, compatible groups of five or six.

AT A GLANCE

- Make sure the mare feels comfortable and safe in a foaling stall.

- Open a mare's Caslick's two weeks prior to the due date.

- "Waxing up" and behavioral changes are signs of impending labor.

- As a mare nears foaling, monitor her closely.

Normal mares in the late stages of pregnancy benefit greatly from daily exercise, and should have ample opportunity to get out and move around freely in good weather. Daily walking helps decrease the buildup of pitting edema in a mare's legs and abdomen during late gestation. It also helps her maintain good muscle tone, an advantage when it comes time for delivery.

The mare ideally has a clean, grassy paddock or field where she can readily be observed in case she decides to foal during the day. A grassy location, free of manure buildup and cleaned by the elements, is a fine place for a mare to foal provided the weather is dry and not too cold. This probably offers a much cleaner environment than her stall. If the mare does foal in a field, it is important for her and the foal to be safe from other horses and to deliver where she will not hurt herself or lose her foal under a fence or into a body of water (tank or pond).

When mares are first brought into their stalls a month or so before foaling, they should be checked for the presence of a Caslick's in the mare's vulva. Mares who have had a Caslick's procedure to prevent pneumovagina (or "wind-sucking") need to have them opened before delivery. Because mares can foal unexpectedly, open a mare's Caslick's when she begins to show signs of increasing udder development or two weeks before her due date, whichever comes first. A mare who attempts to foal through a closed Caslick's in all likelihood will deliver the foal but tear her perineum severely.

Make sure the mare has up-to-date vaccinations at this time. As already stated, the mare concentrates antibodies in her

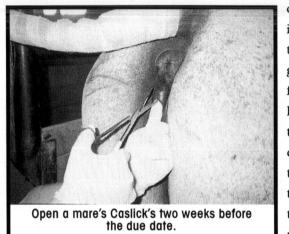

Open a mare's Caslick's two weeks before the due date.

colostrum for the immune protection of the foal. Vaccinations given 30 days before foaling should be tailored by a veterinarian to meet whatever disease problems are typically encountered in the area. Having said this, however, it is prudent to vaccinate all

foaling mares for tetanus, Eastern and Western encephalitis, and influenza. (This regimen is in addition to the rhinopneumonitis prevention regimen of vaccinations for herpes virus at five, seven, and nine months of the gestation.)

Continue deworming programs throughout pregnancy. Make sure to administer anthelmintics that are safe for pregnancy and avoid organophosphate and phenothiazine wormers.

SIGNS OF APPROACHING FOALING

The mare undergoes external body changes in preparation for foaling that the conscientious caretaker can use to help him or her determine when the mare will foal. Although many of the changes we will discuss are considered classic signs, not every mare "reads the book." She might show all, some, or in rare cases even none of the typical signs. Once

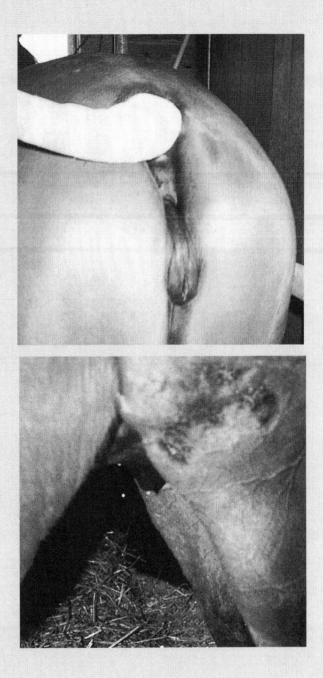

Some of the signs of impending foaling include elongation of the vulva (above) and teats which begin to drip milk.

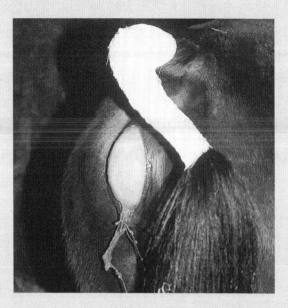

The appearance of the white amnion and discharging allantoic
fluid (above); the foal's forelegs (below) present first in
a normal birth.

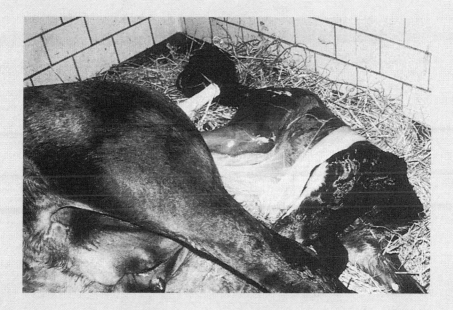

Delivery is nearly complete and the mare and foal rest; (below) they
greet each other for the first time as the bonding process begins.

Allantoic surface (above) and chorionic surface (below) of an equine placenta; a so-called red bag delivery is characterized by presentation of the red chorionic membrane rather than the white amnion.

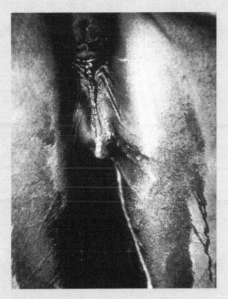

Post-foaling discharge that is pus-tinged (above) is abnormal; ultrasound (below) can be used to detect free fluid in the abdomen in post-foaling mares with hemorrhage or peritonitis.

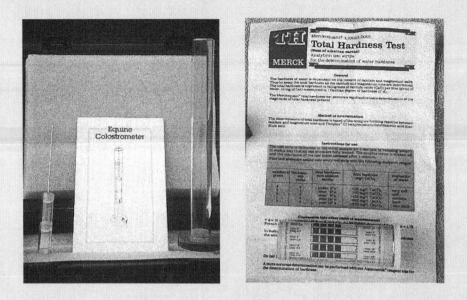

A colostremeter (above, left) measures the quality of colostrum; a milk analysis test (above, right); and an IgG test kit for the foal (below).

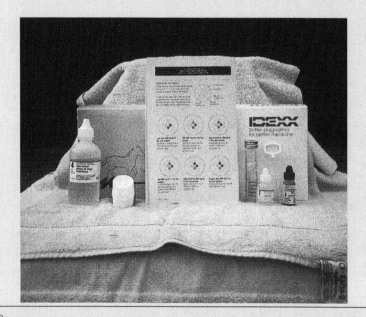

A mare showing rejection behavior toward her foal (above); using a
plank to separate the two while still allowing the foal to nurse can help the
mare learn to accept her newborn.

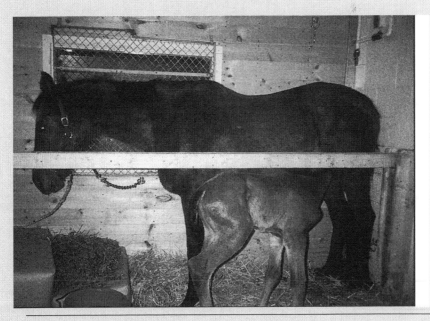

Mares and foals benefit from turn out; always make sure mothers and their youngsters have access to fresh water.

again, observe your mare closely, and keep complete records from year to year. Mares tend to repeat the same outward changes and behaviors at each foaling, and accurate records can help you to outfox her and avoid too many sleepless nights watching the mare watch you watching her not foaling.

About four weeks before foaling, the mare's udder will begin to develop. The mammary gland is divided into two halves. Each half has its own teat, with usually two (but sometimes more) openings for the milk to exit. The udder development begins with the increasing size of the two halves. This initial enlargement is frequently accompanied by localized, pitting edema surrounding the udder, making it appear larger than it is at this early stage. As the development progresses, this edema decreases in most mares, and you can begin to appreciate the true enlargement of the glandular tissues. This enlargement continues until about 48 hours before foaling, when the udder will appear full and somewhat taut.

Up until this point, the teats have remained flat, but during the last 12 to 24 hours they usually begin to fill with colostrum, and a wax-like substance starts to form on the endings. "Waxing up," as it is known, is considered one of the classic signs of impending labor. Waxing can range from the formation of tiny beads of secretion right at

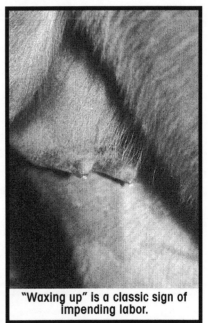

"Waxing up" is a classic sign of impending labor.

the teat endings to large "candles" that project from the teat ends. Remember that not every mare produces this sign in the classic manner, and many mares might wax up days ahead of the actual delivery or never wax at all.

In addition to waxing, many mares also will begin to drip or even stream milk in the final one to four hours before delivery. Some mares will leak milk for days and even weeks prior to delivering, and these mares pose a special concern. Mares who prematurely produce milk lose the valuable colostrum that has built up in their udders in preparation for their foals' needs at birth. The remaining milk frequently has poor antibody content by the time of the actual delivery. If this occurs, attempt to catch the leaking colostrum and save it in the freezer to be bottle or tube fed to the foal. Even better, identify a source of good quality colostrum that has been "banked" (more on this later) for such an occasion. This way, the foal can receive a colostrum supplement shortly after delivery (i.e., within the first one to four hours). In general, the mare who has a fully developed udder and full teats, who is waxed and dripping milk, likely is just hours away from foaling. Remember, though, many mares will foal without demonstrating all of these signs. Maiden mares, though enlarged, frequently will not have a great increase in the size of their udder halves when they first foal compared with the size increase seen in multiparous mares.

The appearance of the mammary gland secretions from the udder changes as foaling draws near. Initially difficult to squeeze out, thin and light straw or serum colored, the secretions become more copious and more milk-like. As colostrum concentrates in the udder, the secretions become readily expressible and often thick with a honey-colored overtone. These changes can occur gradually or within the last hours before delivery.

Likewise, the concentrations of the electrolytes in the mammary secretions shift as the foal matures and delivery draws closer. Calcium (and magnesium) concentrations rise, and sodium and potassium levels fall and rise, respectively, in relation to one another. These changes serve as a subjective measure to help predict how close the mare is to foaling.

Milk calcium concentrations of 40 milligrams per deciliter (mg/dL) or more have been associated with fetal maturity. Commercially available equine milk test kits and/or water quality hardness strips can be used to test the mammary secretions on a daily basis. Most mares demonstrate a rise in milk calcium levels above 40 mg/dL within 48 hours of delivering, although some might demonstrate this change for a considerably longer period before foaling. Therefore, milk calcium levels are a useful, but not an absolute gauge for predicting foaling. A mare whose milk calcium is less than 40mg/dL probably will not foal in the next 24 hours.

Daily laboratory milk analysis can be used to chart the shifts in milk sodium and potassium levels (as well as milk calcium concentrations) to detect when their inversion occurs. Scoring systems using absolute calcium, potassium, and sodium levels, exist that give a quantitative score by which the likelihood that a mare will foal within the next 24 hours can be assessed. As with the other indicative signs, measurement of milk electrolytes helps predict when a mare likely will foal, but are not always absolute.

In preparation for delivery, the ligaments and connective tissues surrounding the mare's pelvis and perineum must become lax so the tissues can stretch and the pelvis widen to accommodate the foal's passage through the birth canal. Evidence of this change is seen in the softening and sinking of the ligaments surrounding the tailhead. This change becomes most pronounced just before delivery when the area over the muscular croup and the line between the tailhead and the point of the buttock become increasingly concave. This change appears more pronounced in mares who have foaled before. But almost every mare will exhibit an appreciable, progressive softening in this area that can be felt during the last week and especially during the few days just before delivery. The tissues of the vulva also become increasingly soft, lax, and filled with edema, a change most noticeable the day the mare delivers. In the final hours before

Some mares seek solitude before foaling.

delivery, the vulva lengthens dramatically. This sign can be subtle and easily missed.

Lastly, many mares will behave differently the last few days before delivery. Rather than staying with the group, many will keep to themselves when out at pasture. Some mares will pace the fence or hang back near the gait, anxious to return to the perceived security of their stall. When in their stall, some mares might act anxious, or conversely become quiet, still, and almost reflective for long periods. Quite a few mares will stop eating in the hours just before labor, while others continue to eat right up to the point of delivery.

Taken together, the signs of mammary development, milk electrolyte changes, pelvic ligament softening, vulvar lengthening, and changes in behavior all indicate that a mare is close to foaling (i.e., within days or hours). But predicting the exact hour she will commence is impossible.

Once it appears that a mare is close to foaling, monitor her around the clock to ensure that help is available if needed. Mares have a good deal of control over labor up to a point. It has been said that "the foal chooses the day of his birth, but the mare chooses the hour." Most mares foal at night. They can shut down stage I labor (provided it hasn't progressed too far) if they become frightened or insecure about their surroundings. They will delay the progression of labor for a few hours until the perceived danger has passed.

Office-to-stall observation windows, video cameras, and monitoring devices all aid in monitoring of the mare. A note of caution about electronic devices: In my opinion, they are useful adjuncts to a foal watch, but should not be relied upon solely. Electronic mechanisms have a way of failing. Some of these devices are triggered by the events of a normal foaling but not an abnormal one and so fail just when their warning is needed most.

Ideally, night checks should be performed every 15 to 20 minutes with as little noise and light changes as possible. Begin these checks in advance of the perceived due date so the watcher's presence during the night will become routine to the mare and not disturb her once her time arrives.

CHAPTER 7

The Normal Foaling

A working knowledge of the equine placenta is important to understand and recognize the events and progression of a normal foaling. The placenta consists of three membranes: the amnion, the allantois, and the chorion (See placental illustration on page 53). The amnion is the white, glistening membrane that covers the foal. The umbilical cord exits the amnion and connects the foal to the allantois. The smooth, gray/white allantois contains the large placental blood vessels that carry the foal's circulating blood from the umbilical chord to the surface of the uterus, then back to the foal via the umbilical chord. The chorion is a velvety red membrane that interlocks in a finger-like way with the entire endometrial surface (i.e., it covers the luminal surface of both uterine horns and the body). Millions of tiny villi covering the chorionic surface give it its characteristic appearance and large, effective surface area over which nutrient, oxygen, and waste ex-

Preparing to foal.

change occur between the developing foal and the mare.

The allantois and chorion are fused, forming what appears to be a single membrane (the chorioallantois), with the chorion facing outward against the uterus, and the allantois facing inward toward the foal. Between the allantoic and amnionic surface is a large, fluid-filled space known as the allantoic cavity. There also is a small amount of fluid within the amnionic cavity surrounding the foal. In effect, the foal at term is contained in a sac (the amnion) within a sac (the chorioallantois), with a large amount of allantoic fluid between the two membranes.

Although parturition (delivery of the foal) is a continuous process, we divide the labor into three stages:

STAGE I LABOR

Stage I labor typically lasts from one to six hours. As uterine contractions strengthen, the foal (who has been lying on its back within the uterus throughout mid-late gestation) is stimulated to rotate and spiral around from a curled up, upside down position to a right side up position with both forelegs and head and neck extended ("diver's position"). The foal's failure to achieve this normal delivery position could indicate a foal that is weak and compromised in some manner, and might require extra nursing care upon delivery.

As uterine contractions increase in strength and frequency, they cause the membranes and the foal to put increasing pressure on the "ripened" cervix, making it dilate. Inwardly these activities cause varying degrees of pain and discomfort to the mare, which she outwardly manifests. Many mares become restless and walk around their stall switching and elevating their tails. They might demonstrate mild colic signs: pawing, looking at their flanks, stretching out, getting up and down, Flehman (lip curling), etc. Many mares will break out in a light sweat, especially on their chest and behind their elbows and on their flanks. Some mares will demonstrate anorexia, but others will continue to eat small amounts of hay early on in between pacing, and some mares will defecate frequently.

As the cervix stretches, there is a neuroendocrine response that releases the hormone oxytocin from the brain (Ferguson's Reflex). In addition to strengthening the uterine contractions, oxytocin also will cause milk to let down, and it is at this point that some mares begin to leak colostrum from their teats.

Closely observe the mare without disturbing her. Most mares would prefer to foal unobserved (and many do). Remember that the mare can and will delay stage I labor if she is upset about her environment. When a mare is suspected to be very close or actually in stage I labor, her stall should be quietly cleaned of any manure piles and rebedded with fresh straw. If it is not too disturbing to her, her tail can be wrapped and her perineum washed at this time. It might be less disruptive, however, if she is just maintained in a well-groomed condition each evening and only disturbed if she is grossly conta-

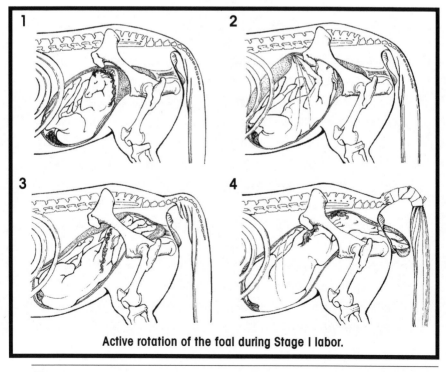

Active rotation of the foal during Stage I labor.

minated or needs examination by knowledgeable attendants because of an abnormal progression of events.

As stage I progresses and the cervix becomes increasingly dilated, the chorioallantois begins to bulge into the birth canal and finally ruptures under the increasing pressure of the allantoic fluid and/or the forelimbs of the foal. This fetal membrane rupture releases the allantoic fluid. Normally amber colored and odorless, this fluid's release can range from a sudden gush of fluid to a small, frequent trickle. Again, the mare needs to be watched closely or this event can be missed or mistaken for urination. Stage I labor ends with this "breaking of the water."

STAGE II LABOR

Stage II labor, the active expulsion of the foal, usually lasts between five to 40 minutes. Within five minutes of the initial rupture of the chorioallantois and release of the allantoic fluid, the glistening, white amnion should appear at the vulvar lips. Delay or failure of the amnion to appear indicates that the foal is malpositioned and that the mare needs to be examined as quickly as possible. If the red chorion appears instead of the white amnion, this indicates premature separation of the placental attachment to the uterus, endangering the foal's oxygen supply. It is imperative that if this "red bag delivery" is observed, the chorioallantois be opened immediately so that the foal in its amnion can be delivered rapidly through this opening. Once delivered, the foal's head must be cleared of the amnion and its breathing stimulated (receiving oxygen and resuscitation if needed) as quickly as possible. Foals which have experienced premature separation of the placenta are in danger of becoming "dummy foals" and require close monitoring.

In a normal foaling, the bubble of the amnion is followed quickly by the appearance of one foot, then the second foot, and then the nose of the foal. By presenting one foot at a time, the foal reduces the diameter of its shoulders, making it easier for the mare to pass the shoulders through her pelvis. The feet should be pointed heel side down. Heel side up indicates either a backward delivery (i.e., hind feet first) or a foal that is upside down.

During stage I labor, the mare does not show signs of active straining, but as the foal engages the cervix and birth canal of the vagina and pelvis, the mare is stimulated to push. The hallmark of stage II labor is active abdominal contractions. Straining is intermittent with rest periods of two to four minutes between bursts of two to eight contractions. Progress should be made with each series of contractions. Lack of progress is cause for concern.

Most mares will get up and down once or twice and reposition themselves, then lie on their sides to deliver the foal. Occasionally a mare will remain standing, requiring her attendants to catch and hold the foal as it is delivered. The most forceful contractions frequently are those occurring with the passage of the head and then the shoulders, and the mare often will pause to rest after each becomes free of the vulva.

Once the foal's hips have passed through the vulva, the mare usually will lie quietly for several minutes with the foal's hind legs still in her. At this point it is important to make sure the foal's head is free of the amnion and that it is breathing. Note whether there is any meconium staining the foal within the amnion. A normal foal is clean, but stressed foals might defecate during delivery and be covered with meconium. This "fetal diarrhea" is also a sign that a foal will likely require assistance and medical care.

Disturb the mare as little as possible and allow her and the foal to have a few minutes to recover from the delivery and lie quietly with the umbilical cord still attached. It has long been thought that a portion of the foal's blood supply (up to 20%) remained in the placenta after delivery. Leaving the umbilical attachment undisturbed was considered important so uterine contractions on the placenta would "pump" the remaining blood back into the foal. It is now unclear whether this actually occurs, but it is probably wise not to break the umbilical attachment prematurely. The magical moment of foaling occurs when the new foal takes its first look at the new world and is discovered by its dam. Frequently they will nicker at each other and the mare will reach around to touch her foal muzzle to muzzle.

Allow the mare the chance to lick her foal; intervene to help dry the foal only if it is extremely cold. The mare and foal need to bond, and any interference, no matter how well intentioned, can damage the pairing and potentially lead to the mare rejecting her foal (especially if the mare is a maiden). Resist the urge to participate in this moment. Once the foal begins to struggle, the mare usually will get to her feet and come around to inspect her baby more thoroughly. The umbilical cord will be broken naturally at this time.

STAGE III LABOR

Stage III labor is the passage of the fetal membranes. Expulsion usually occurs within an hour, but the placenta is not considered retained until three hours after the foal's birth. After the foal is delivered, the uterus continues to have contractions. The microvilli on the chorionic surface of the placenta "release" or "unlock" from their connection with the endometrium, and the placenta is expelled from the uterus. The chorioallantois usually is turned inside out as it is dropped. Some mares will become crampy during this process and show signs of colic; others will lie down quietly as they work on passing the membranes. Still others are busy taking care of their foals and show no outward sign of discomfort.

Some mares might become uncomfortable enough during this process to require walking or low-dose analgesics to help them through it. Remember to view any mare showing abnormal signs of discomfort after foaling with concern, and to consult with a veterinarian. Until the mare passes the mem-

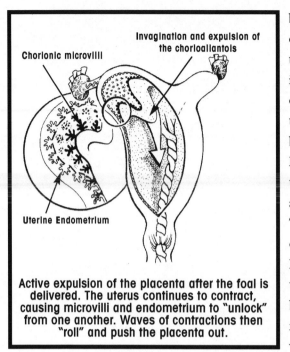

Chorionic microvilli

Invagination and expulsion of the chorioallantois

Uterine Endometrium

Active expulsion of the placenta after the foal is delivered. The uterus continues to contract, causing microvilli and endometrium to "unlock" from one another. Waves of contractions then "roll" and push the placenta out.

branes, tie up the placenta to itself carefully to keep the mare from inadvertently stepping on it. Never apply traction to the placenta because you can severely damage the mare's uterus. Just let gravity and the mare work on it. The placenta will slide out of the mare once it has released from the uterus, and there should be no straining on the mare's part. (A mare which continues to strain after her foal has been delivered should be examined immediately as she might have a previously undetected twin or might be trying to prolapse her uterus.) Once the placenta has been passed, it should be examined for abnormalities and to make sure it is intact. The chorioallantois most likely will be turned inside out, with the gray-white allantoic surface with its large vessels facing outward.

Carefully check to see that both horns of the placenta are complete and that there are no missing portions on the placenta. Take especially good care to examine the tips of each horn, where the placenta is most likely to be retained. The only opening in the chorioallatois should be at the base of the body (bottom of the "T"). This is where the foal exited.

While handling the placenta and checking the horns, you frequently will encounter a soft, tan-gray mass of tissue that is free within the allantoic cavity. This is the Hippomane, a solid mass of cells that is a normal finding and not cause for alarm. As you examine the allantoic surface, the umbilical cord and amnion will be fully visible as well.

Next, turn the placenta right side out so that the red chorion is facing outward and check the entire surface to ensure that it is complete. At this time, you also are looking for any gross discolorations or abnormal thickenings. The chorion should appear a rich red. The only normal exceptions to this are the normal avillous pale areas that correspond to where the placenta was in contact with the cervix and the tiny openings of the oviducts at the tips of each horn. The "cervical star" will appear as pale striations radiating from the opening in the base of the body of the placenta. There frequently will also be pale linear areas (particularly close to the base of the horns) that correspond to where the chorion was folded on itself. Lastly, the placenta should be weighed. The normal placenta is about 10% of the foal's birth weight (10 to 12 pounds for an average 100-pound foal). Any abnormalities should be brought to a veterinarian's attention. Heavy or discolored placentas could indicate a placentitis, which might require medical treatment for the foal and mare. An incomplete placenta or one that has been retained for more than three hours is a medical emergency, and a veterinarian should be contacted at once.

CHAPTER 8

Complications of Late Pregnancy and Delivery

In general, most late-term mares will accumulate some degree of edema on their abdomens and stock up in their hind limbs in much the same manner as a pregnant woman with swollen ankles. The weight of the developing foal and its surrounding fluids causes increasing pressure on the veins that drain the ventral abdomen, which in turn causes fluid to pool in the tissues, resulting in a pitting edema that can be felt and in many cases seen. Typically this edema is most obvious at the lowest point of the belly and around the udder, but it can extend all the way from the flanks to the elbows and become quite thick.

In some instances, the edema formation can become extreme. Any condition that increases the weight on the mare's abdomen beyond what is normally encountered during late gestation (i.e., twin pregnancy, fetal hydrops, etc.) will exacerbate this condition. Sometimes older mares will accumulate an impressive degree of edema without any discernable predisposing reason. Mares which are confined also frequently develop excessive edema. The concern in these extreme conditions is that the weight will exceed the abdominal tissues' ability to support it and the mare will rupture her prepubic tendon or other abdominal musculature. Prepubic tendon ruptures occur rarely in all breeds, but draft breed mares are over represented in those cases that occur.

Mares with impending rupture have abdominal pain, are reluctant to move, and have increased abdominal edema and swelling, especially around the point of tissue damage. Attempts to manage the condition and prevent rupture via anti-inflammatories, belly wraps, limiting exertional stress to the tissues, and decreasing dietary roughage

AT A GLANCE

• Late-term mares showing signs of colic could have a uterine torsion.

• Rapid recognition and correction of dystocia is critical.

• A retained placenta can lead to laminitis.

• Uterine artery rupture is a potential foaling complication in older mares.

have limited success. Such attempts should be made only in those situations in which the foal is viable and close to term and of greater value than the mare. Mares which have ruptured their prepubic tendon have a characteristic appearance. As the tendon gives way, the belly drops and the mare's udder pulls forward. Loss of the abdominal musculature attachments destabilizes the pelvis and it assumes an abnormal angle.

Once rupture has occurred, the mare's chances are grim. Attempts at surgical repair seldom succeed, and the mare usually faces euthanasia. Therapy to save the mare before the rupture or in cases where partial rupture has occurred is aimed at removing the stress on the abdomen. This means terminating the pregnancy by inducing parturition and delivering the foal regardless of its state of development. If the foal is viable after delivery, a decision can be made as to whether to institute veterinary care or to euthanize, depending on the foal's condition and value. In many cases the mare needs help during delivery as she cannot generate enough abdominal press. A mare which has had a near or partial rupture should not be bred back.

UTERINE TORSION

Uterine torsion (a twisting of the uterus around its long axis) sometimes is seen in mares during the last trimester, usually before but sometimes at term. The twist can be anywhere from 180 to 540 degrees in either direction, and is thought to result from the foal bouncing inside the uterus, the dam rolling, or an unfortunate combination of the two. The uterus and the foal become increasingly compromised depending on how badly twisted the tissues are. The tighter the twist, the more cut off the uterine blood supply becomes. Death of the foal and uterine rupture could occur in cases that are severe, longstanding, or both. Initially the mare might show only signs of mild colic that persist and/or reappear after medication. A gastrointestinal (GI) source for the pain has to be ruled out, but frequently mares with a uterine torsion will continue to pass feces. Mares which have more severe twists and/or a piece of bowel caught up in the twist might exhibit severe and violent colic signs initially. As the foal and the uterine tissues begin to die, the mare could become depressed and "shocky" as her condition likewise deteriorates and peritonitis sets in.

Any late-term mare exhibiting signs of colic is suspect for this condition and should be examined by a veterinarian. Diagnosis is made on rectal examination. Early diagnosis is key to saving the mare and the foal. The torsion can be corrected by rolling an anesthetized mare or performing standing flank surgery in cooperative individuals. If the condition is corrected early and care is initiated before tissue compromise occurs, the pregnancy frequently will progress normally.

DYSTOCIA

Dystocia is an abnormal delivery. Any foaling that results in an injury to the dam or compromise of the foal and/or requires assistance is a dystocia. Rapid recognition and correction of dystocia is critical for two major reasons. First, delivery is an explosive event. The mare musters tremendous force in her abdominal press and delivery is rapid. Therefore, the potential for self injury to the mare is high if there is any fetal malposition-ing. The mare lit-erally will push the foal through any obstructing tissues (uterus, vagina, rectum) in her effort to deliver it, damag-ing herself, and compromising her reproductive capa-

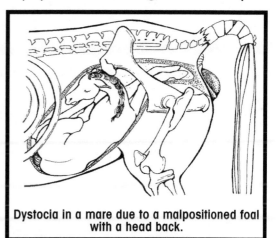

Dystocia in a mare due to a malpositioned foal with a head back.

bilities. Secondly, the mare's placenta rapidly begins to detach during the delivery process. Normally, stage II labor (expulsion of the foal) is accomplished in 20 to 40 minutes. Any delay in delivery beyond this frequently results in com-promise or loss of the foal as the placenta detaches partially or fully and the foal's oxygen supply is cut off with the foal still inside the mare.

Never discount the importance of being present and able to recognize when a foaling is abnormal. Any delay in the normal sequence of events, deviations from the foal's normal positioning, or failure of the mare to make steady progress toward delivery with each effort is cause for concern and warrants immediate veterinary attention.

Examples of when to be concerned and call for help include (but are not limited to):

1) A mare which has been demonstrating signs of first stage labor for more than an hour but does not show any sign of progressing to stage II.

2) A mare which begins to exert abdominal straining without "breaking her water" — beware of premature separa-tion of the allantochorion and a "red bag" delivery.

3) Failure of the white amnion to appear at the vulva

within five minutes of the water breaking.

4) Failure of both front feet and the nose to appear in the expected fashion, the appearance of more than two feet, or the front feet being upside down or the hind feet presented.

5) Failure of the mare to make progress delivering the foal even if the foal's outward positioning appears normal.

6) Failure of the mare to make any abdominal effort even though the foal appears properly presented.

7) Appearance of the foal's head or a limb through the anus instead of the vulva.

8) Meconium staining of the amnionic fluid noticeable through the white membrane as the amnion presents. (Again, facilitating rapid delivery is indicated.)

9) Frank hemorrhage from the mare's vulva.

The constant rule is, if in doubt call for experienced help. In the meantime, the most important thing you can do to help your mare and foal is to remain calm. Your calm demeanor will reassure the mare, and she is more likely to let you help her. If the foal is obviously malpositioned (i.e., leg back, failure to make progress) the best thing you can do is try to keep the mare from straining further. This is best accomplished by getting the mare up and keeping her walking in an open area until the veterinarian arrives. This sometimes is easier said than done as the mare will want to lie down with each contraction and push with the stimulus of the foal in the birth canal. Some mares occasionally will become violent with the pain, so use caution to avoid placing yourself or anyone else in a dangerous position.

Once the veterinarian arrives, he or she will perform a brief, pointed physical on the mare to assess her vital signs and overall condition, then will move quickly to examine the reproductive tract. The tail is wrapped and the perineum thoroughly cleaned before the vaginal exam begins. The mare will require some restraint during this exam. Most mares respond better with a minimal amount of restraint in the form of a halter and shank and sometimes a twitch.

The use of sedatives and epidural anesthesia is at the discretion of the attending veterinarian, and will likely be employed only if the mare is extremely fractious or straining too hard to permit examination and manipulation.(Sedation of the mare also means sedation of a possibly compromised foal. A mare which has had an epidural might not be able to push effectively, and therefore will be of little to no help when the foal is in a correct position for expulsion.)

The veterinarian will assess the mare carefully to discern stage of labor, degree of cervical dilation, membrane rupture, the presence of any injuries to the mare's tract, size of the birth canal/bony pelvis relative to the size of the foal, position of the foal, and whether the foal is still alive. Fetal malposition is the most common reason for dystocia in the mare. A malformed foal also might be difficult to deliver. Unlike cattle, equine dystocias rarely are caused by a foal that is too large to pass through the mare's pelvis unless a previous injury has decreased the mare's pelvic diameter.

Once the veterinarian has examined the mare and identified the cause of the problem, he or she then will determine how best to proceed. Depending on the cause of the dystocia, this could range from simply adding lubrication and repositioning a limb to administering general anesthesia and elevating the mare's hindquarters to allow more extensive manipulations. Severe cases of malpositioning and a live foal might mandate a Caesarean section. If the foal is already dead, a fetotomy (dismemberment of the dead foal within the mare and delivery piecemeal) might be performed.

Mares requiring anesthesia, a fetotomy, and/or surgery are frequently better served by referral to a clinic that handles such emergencies. Fortunately, many dystocias are resolved on the farm. Anyone assisting the veterinarian with a dystocia must remember that all manipulations must be performed as quickly as possible and that all equipment and lubricants must be kept clean of contaminants (bedding, manure, etc.)

to minimize the contamination inevitable during manipulations within the mare's tract. If traction is required to deliver the foal after any malposition is corrected, it is important not to use excessive force. Too much force can injure the foal and/or the mare's tract. (Traction should not exceed a maximum of two to three adults using obstetrical ropes or chains on the foal's head and limbs or direct grasping of the legs on the cannons above the fetlocks).

When in doubt, use more lubrication and massage and stretch the vulva, allowing a little time for the mare's soft tissues to stretch as the foal's head and shoulders are passed. Pull when the mare strains (her pelvic diameter is at its widest then) and maintain tension when she rests so the foal does not slip back. Initially pull straight back and as the shoulders and ribs clear the vulva, direct the pulling force downward toward the mare's hocks. Pulling in this fashion works with the bend of the foal's body and the curve of the mare's birth canal. Once the foal's hips have cleared, traction on the foal can cease. Everyone can rest provided the foal does not require resuscitation, its head is free of the amnion, and it is breathing normally. To quote Dr. Robert Hillman, the most important points to remember when assisting a foaling are, "Be clean, be gentle, and use lots of lube."

RETAINED PLACENTA

Retention of the placenta after foaling is a medical emergency in the mare. Retention of even a tiny piece of the chorioallantois, or even a patch of chorionic microvilli, is enough to cause delayed uterine involution and form a nidus for bacterial endometritis.

The exact mechanism by which the placenta detaches from the uterus is not fully understood. But it is thought that separation occurs when blood flow through the umbilical vessels ceases, which collapses the chorionic villi. Uterine contractions continue during stage III labor. These contractions effectively decrease uterine size and further "unlock" the chorionic villi from their interdigitation with the uterine crypts. In addition, the uterine contractions act to push the detaching placenta out of the uterine lumen in a propulsive fashion. The "waves" start at the tips of the horns and flow into the body, ending at the cervix. In this manner the chorioallantois is released beginning at the tip of the horns and is rolled inside out (or allantoic surface outward) as it is expelled. As the placenta passes through the cervix, the mare once again might be stimulated to push, but seldom shows outward signs of concerted straining. As the placenta passes through the lips of the vulva, gravity also begins to work on

the weight of the dangling portion, adding mild traction to the process. Once the placenta fully detaches, it usually slips to the ground in a sudden rush, seemingly unnoticed by the mare.

Placentas are retained in approximately 2% to 10% of foaling

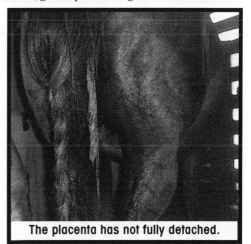

The placenta has not fully detached.

mares. While not fully understood, possible causes of retained placentas include any swelling in the microvilli (uterine or placental) that "locks" them together, poor or absent uterine contractions perhaps caused by hormonal imbalances, and/or low blood calcium at the time of foaling. In many cases of retained placenta, the chorioallantois is retained at or near the tip of the non-pregnant horn, and either the whole placenta will hang partially from the mare with the rest remaining inside the mare's tract or the attached portion will be torn away as the placenta tears free. This tearing will leave an abnormal hole in the membranes that is discovered during examination of the placenta. Retention of chorionic villi could be a subtle finding during a placental examination.

Leaving behind a small piece is just as bad as having the whole placenta inside the mare. Potential complications include toxemia (a release of cellular and/or bacterial endotoxins into the mare's bloodstream), septicemia (bacterial infection spreading to the generalized circulation), laminitis, permanent damage to the uterine lining (endometrium), and even death. Prompt medical therapy can improve the chances for the mare's long-term reproductive health, soundness, and overall survival. Veterinary attention should be sought if there is any question that the placenta might have been retained. Treatment is aimed at causing the retained membranes to be expelled by improving uterine contractility (oxytocin), protecting the mare from bacterial infection (broad spectrum antibiotics) and endotoxemia (Banamine), overall systemic support (IV fluids), and protecting and addressing the feet for any possible development of laminitis (frog support, IV DMSO, vasodilators that are not counterproductive to uterine tone).

The veterinarian might recommend cleansing the uterus with sterile saline before and after expulsion of the placenta. Manual removal of the placenta is not recommended because of the potential for causing hemorrhage and thrombosis, damaging the endometrium, and leaving chorionic villi behind. Use extreme care when handling the dangling portion of the placenta while tying it to avoid placing sudden, forceful traction on it. Never pull on the retained placenta. Great potential exists for doing permanent damage to the mare's uterus and compromising her future fertility. Most retained placentas respond to therapy within a few hours and are released, but some will remain attached for days before finally letting go.

Untreated, a mare's condition will deteriorate over 24 to 48 hours. She will become depressed and febrile, back off eating, and stop caring for her foal. As she becomes increasingly toxic, her gums will redden and darken and laminitis will set in. Early signs of laminitis include increased heat in the feet, a palpable bounding digital pulse, and lameness. Foundering horses usually will become lame first in their front feet and characteristically will rock their weight back onto their hind feet. When walking, they will land heel first with their front feet to avoid weight on their toes. They often will be reluctant to move or pick up their feet when asked, and prefer to lie down rather than stand. Any mare demonstrating any of these signs after foaling requires immediate attention.

How rapidly these signs set in and how severe they become is determined in large part by the virulence of the organism residing in the uterus. I have seen some mares which appeared only mildly affected by a placenta that was retained 24 hours and another mare which literally sank out of her hoof walls within 24 hours of foaling. Once it appears that the mare has retained her placenta, seek veterinary assistance immediately. Delaying treatment poses a risk because it is difficult to predict how the condition might affect the mare.

With good, supportive care and immediate therapy to control the infection, endotoxemia, and possible laminitis, most mares recover fully and are reproductively sound even if their placenta is retained over several days.

PERINEAL LACERATIONS

The tremendous force of uterine contractions and abdominal press during foaling poses great potential for damage to the soft tissues of the mare's reproductive tract. Nature has provided some protection to the mare's delicate structures in the form of thick tissue pads that cover the soles and sharp edges of the unborn foal's hooves ("angels' slippers"). Further, the slippery amnion and allantoic fluid lubricate the foal and the birth canal, respectively, and facilitate the foal's passage. Even so, failure of the mare's tract to stretch and dilate adequately, or malpositioning of the foal's head and/or limbs, could bruise and tear the mare's uterus, cervix, vagina, rectum, vulva, and perineum. Also any potential ridge of tissue (i.e., an incompletely opened Caslick's, tight vestibulo-vaginal junction, or partial hymen) creates an edge on which a foal's foot might catch and cause a tear as the mare pushes the foal through the soft tissue obstruction. Maiden foaling mares seem particularly prone to lacerations of the vagina, rectum, and perineum, as these tissues never have stretched before. Tight vestibulo-vaginal junctions also increase this risk.

Perineal lacerations are divided into three categories based on their severity. First-degree perineal lacerations involve only the skin and mucosa at the top edge of the vulvar opening (the dorsal commissure). These tears result from a failure of the tissues to stretch adequately to permit passage of the foal's poll and shoulders, and the dorsal commissure instead tears during the delivery.

Second-degree perineal lacerations are a tearing through the mucosa of the roof of the vestibule/caudal vagina into the perineal body and out through the dorsal commissure of the vulva, creating a tear that dissects up to but not into the anal ring. Second-degree perineal lacerations occur as the foal's feet become hooked on the vestibulo-vaginal junction and plow through the tissues as the mare pushes the foal on out. This can occur even though the foal is in the normal "diver's" position for delivery, but is even more likely to occur if the foal has hooked one or both of its feet up behind its ears and over its head.

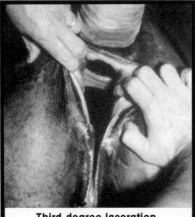

Third-degree laceration.

Third-degree perineal lacerations occur in the same manner as second-degree lacerations, but instead of the foal's foot merely raking the roof of the vestibule, it is pushed up through the roof and into the mare's rectum. If the foal is able to retract its foot back into the birth canal before the mare's next effort to push it out, then a recto-vaginal fistula is formed by the hole created between the mare's rectum and vestibule/caudal vagina. If, however, the foal does not retract its limb from the rectum, the foot (and/or sometimes the head) then will exit through the anus. As the rest of the foal is passed, all of the tissue between the opening of the anus and the dorsal commissure of the vulva will be torn out.

Minor tears that might predispose the mare to pneumovagina can be sewn and the mare's vulva sutured right after she foals and before tissue swelling has had a chance to form. In the case of second- and third-degree perineal lacerations and recto-vaginal fistulas, tissue damage, bruising, and swelling usually are severe enough at the time of injury that repair has to wait. Bruised and swollen tissue will not hold suture well, and any attempt to repair the tissues will break down. Elective surgery to repair these injuries usually is performed four to eight weeks after foaling.

Bruising and tears to the mare's cervix likely occur when the foal passes through an incompletely dilated cervix, or a dilated cervix that must open even farther to allow passage of a large foal. Again, the tissues are asked to stretch beyond their limits and tear. This situation also can be caused by overzealous and hasty attendants who apply traction to deliver the foal rapidly before the cervix has had a chance to dilate completely.

The major concern over cervical tears concerns the damaged cervix's ability to form an adequate seal during subsequent diestrous periods. Destruction of the diestrous cervical barrier severely compromises the mare's fertility, as her cervical lumen and uterus are more vulnerable to contamination and resultant inflammation and ascending infections. Cervical tears usually are identified at the mare's postpartum check. The torn cervix is re-examined once the mare is in diestrus and assessed for the seal's competency. If the cervix can form a tight seal, no further repair is warranted. If the seal is judged inadequate, surgical repair can be attempted once all swelling and bruising of the tissues have resolved. Once torn, a cervix is likely to tear again at subsequent foalings because the scar tissue is not as resilient as normal tissue.

Uterine tears can occur because of a malpositioned foal, obstetrical manipulations, injury to the uterus during uterine lavage, as a result of a uterine torsion, or in the course of an otherwise apparently normal foaling. This is a life-threatening injury to the mare because of the potential complications of herniation of bowel through the torn uterus, resultant peritonitis, and/or hemorrhage. Mares which tear during stage II labor might abruptly stop pushing and become rapidly shocky (outwardly they are cold to the touch, sweaty, etc). Conversely, mares may deliver their foal, then go on to show signs ranging from acute to gradually developing colic, no vulvar discharge to frank vulvar hemorrhage, severe depression, or possibly no outward signs for 12 to 24 hours.

Any mare not acting normally during the postpartum period should be examined by a veterinarian as soon as possible. Uterine body tears might be identified by direct palpation of the uterine wall via the vagina, but tears elsewhere in the uterus most likely will be unreachable in the immediately post-partum uterus. In that event, your veterinarian will be able to make a presumptive diagnosis based on the mare's clinical signs and examination of contaminated peritoneal fluid. This fluid is obtained by placing a needle or teat canula through the mare's ventral body wall and into her abdomen to collect the fluid (abdominocentesis). Immediate abdominal surgical repair of the uterine laceration (along with good supportive care, anti-inflammatories and antibiotics) is indicated to give the best chance of saving the mare's life and future fertility.

COMPLICATIONS IN OLDER MARES

As broodmares age, the potential for complications associated with pregnancy and labor naturally increases. A common problem encountered in the aged broodmare is a sometimes fatal rupture and hemorrhage of one of the arteries supplying the uterus (frequently it is the right middle uterine artery). Rupture can occur anytime during late gestation — especially if the mare is excited or stressed — and into the early post-partum period, but it typically occurs at foaling. As the pregnancy progresses, stress increases on the walls of the uterine arteries as blood flow through the arteries increases.

Older mares can have complications.

During labor the internal blood pressure acutely increases, adding more strain on internal vessel walls. There is additional pressure on the outside of the vessel walls as the vessels (which course along on either side of the uterus within the broad ligaments) are stretched and compressed between the foal and the pelvis during the birthing process.

Possible reasons why these arteries rupture in some mares include: 1) Degenerative "old age" changes within the arteries themselves; 2) Low relative serum copper levels. (Adequate copper levels are necessary for normal vessel elasticity. Older mares in general and mares which rupture their uterine arteries in particular have been shown in one study to have lower copper levels overall when compared to young mares or age matched unaffected mares.); 3) Increased broad ligament and uterine artery tension due to left-sided uterine displacement caused by a full cecum.

Rupture of the uterine artery could result in rapid, extensive blood loss and death if hemorrhage occurs directly into the abdominal cavity. If bleeding is contained within the broad ligament and under the adjacent uterine serosa, a hematoma and subsequent clot could form, containing and stopping the hemorrhage. Mares which bleed directly into their abdomens demonstrate signs of rapidly developing shock: pale mucous membranes (gums), rapid heart rates, rapid respiratory rates, and cold sweat. They might exhibit signs of colic as well and die fairly quickly.

Mares whose bleeding is contained within the broad ligament experience pain and act colicky as tension and stretch is applied to the tissues by the dissecting and enlarging hematoma and resultant clot. Pain increases the heart and respiratory rates. Signs of colic caused by hematoma formation might be subtle, start off mildly, and be mistaken for foaling "after cramps." Any mare which becomes colicky during or after foaling needs close monitoring. If the colic fails to subside or increases in severity, the mare should be examined by a veterinarian as quickly as possible.

Little can be done to save mares which have rapid bleeding into their abdomens. In general, mares which die do so within the first 24 hours of foaling, but death can occur up to several weeks afterward if the clot is disturbed and bleeding recurs. Fatalities occur most typically in mares 18 years or older, whereas non-fatal clot formation is more typical in affected mares 11 to 15 years of age.

A veterinarian will make the diagnosis based on the mare's clinical signs, by direct rectal palpation of the hematoma in the broad ligament, and sometimes by abdominocentesis. For mares which have survived the initial bleeding, treatment is aimed at keeping them as calm as possible. The attending veterinarian might choose to administer sedative drugs. If the mare's blood count becomes severely low, the veterinarian might administer IV fluids, plasma, or blood transfusions. In general, though, transfusions do not seem to alter the final outcome in these cases and actually can be harmful if they excite or agitate the mare during their administration. Surgery usually is a last-ditch effort to save a valuable mare which is already at a veterinary hospital. If the mare survives, it is recommended that she not be bred back.

Mares which have bled before likely will do so again with subsequent pregnancies. The likelihood that they will die also increases. Management practices that might decrease the risk of uterine artery rupture in older broodmares include feeding less dry roughage (i.e., hay) in the days just before foaling in an effort to decrease the size of the cecum by decreasing gut fill. Avoiding stressful situations (floating teeth, vanning, strenuous exercise) in late gestation or just after foaling also can help. It might help to monitor copper levels in "at risk" older mares (especially those 15 years or older), and adjust dietary minerals accordingly with the help of an equine nutritionist and your veterinarian so that the diet meets an individual mare's needs and remains balanced. Checking for low blood copper levels, especially in the last month of gestation, also might help identify at-risk mares which warrant especially close monitoring at foaling time. Lining up a nurse mare might not be a bad idea in case the dam has a problem.

GASTROINTESTINAL PROBLEMS

A gastrointestinal cause of abdominal pain needs to be ruled out in all horses demonstrating signs of colic (flank watching, kicking at belly, rolling, depression, decreased appetite, wringing/elevating the tailhead, etc.). Foaling mares are susceptible to a number of labor-related GI complications. These include cecal and large colon ruptures, large colon volvulus (twisted gut), small colon contusions and ruptures, herniated

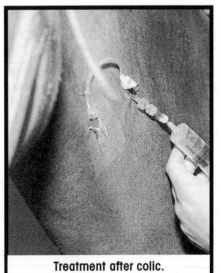

Treatment after colic.

small bowel secondary to uterine or cranial vaginal tears, impactions, and rectal constipation.

The force generated during stage II labor is strong enough to contuse and/or rupture the mare's large or small bowel if it becomes caught between the mare's pelvis and uterus containing the foal while she strains. Contusions can cause mild colic that subsides as the intestine heals, or they can result in portions of badly devitalized bowel that cause peritonitis and increasing signs of depression, pain, and toxemia. Ruptured bowel causes severe peritonitis and septic shock within four to six hours. Surgery can save horses with devitalized bowel if the lesion is accessible, not too extensive, and operated on early enough.

Mares which have already ruptured their bowel have little hope of survival because horses cannot cope with the resultant peritonitis. The humane recourse is to euthanize these mares as soon as the presumptive diagnosis is confirmed via abdominal tap and evaluation of the peritoneal fluid or through exploratory surgery.

Although the reason(s) remains unclear, broodmares seem susceptible to developing large colon torsions during the first 100 days after foaling. A twisted colon compromises its blood supply, and the intestines distend with gas over time. These horses usually are in a lot of pain and want to lie down. They often will be quite bloated, increasing the chance of a rupture, and they rapidly succumb to shock.

Uterine tears already have been discussed. When an opening in the uterus exists, there is potential for small bowel to herniate through it. Herniated bowel might become severely constricted and devitalized. Herniated bowel also might become grossly contaminated with bacteria when exposed to the uterine or vaginal lumens or the outside air if it exits the vulva.

Impactions in post-foaling mares can result from abnormal peristalsis or ilius in a portion of bowel that may have been contused (small colon impactions secondary to contusions especially). Impactions also can be a result of consuming too much roughage and/or dehydration around the time of foaling.

Decreased manure production is an early and significant sign of a problem in these cases. Most mares voluntarily decrease their own hay consumption in the days before foaling, but as previously discussed, it is a good management practice to feed less hay at this time. Laxative feeds such as grass and bran mashes also can help prevent post-foaling impactions. Mildly salting the feed to encourage water consumption also can help, and providing plenty of clean, fresh water at a palatable temperature is vital. Having a veterinarian administer mineral oil in an impaction-prone mare before she foals is another good way to anticipate and ward off a problem. (This requires a judgment call to weigh the risk of upsetting the mare by the tubing process during late pregnancy.)

Post-foaling mares can experience simple constipation, especially if there has been a lot of bruising and hematoma formation in the tissues of the vagina and perineum. It is painful for these mares to defecate, so they resist and become constipated. Again, laxative feeds, and even cold compresses (initially) and topical use of ointments such as Preparation H™ might help these mares become comfortable enough to continue to pass feces. Judicious and restrained use of anti-inflammatory drugs such as Banamine (Flunixin Meglumine) at the discretion of a veterinarian also might help decrease the pain and inflammation in the perineal tissues in moderately to severely bruised mares.

CHAPTER 9

Care of the Mare and Foal

During the first 12 to 48 hours post foaling, the mare should be watched closely. As previously discussed, mares which appear colicky or depressed should receive immediate veterinary attention. The normal post-foaling mare will be bright, alert, and responsive to people and her surroundings. She will take an active interest in her foal, and will nurse it frequently. The mare will be attentive and protective, standing with her head over the foal as it sleeps. (Stabled mares often continue to eat hay as they stand over the foal and end up half burying their sleeping foal under dropped wisps!) She will place herself between her foal and any perceived threat from other animals, horses, or people. She will be comfortable and her vital signs (heart rate, respiratory rate, pulse quality, and mucous membrane color) will be stable and normal.

Unless the mare shows signs of a serious problem, physical examination of her reproductive tract is limited to visually examining her perineum for tears or abnormal discharge so as not to disturb the course of early involution or introduce infection to the recovering reproductive tract. Mares with serious perineal conformation flaws which necessitate a Caslick's procedure to keep them from "wind-sucking" may be resutured by a veterinarian in the immediate hour after delivery unless there is major swelling of the surrounding tissues. Mares which have swelling and/or are not severely afflicted by pneumovagina if left unsutured may be repaired as needed at the seven-day post-foaling examination or later once tissue bruising and swelling have subsided and the tissues will hold suture.

A complete placental examination should be performed to ensure that there are no abnormalities and that the passed placenta is complete. Many post-partum mares are tired from the strain of carrying the foal through the last days of the gestation and the effort of delivery. Many will lie down beside their foal after the first few hours and sleep. This is normal, but any mare who spends long periods down should be examined for any indication that her feet are becoming sore (laminitis/founder) or for other abnormalities that would cause her to be recumbent.

Normal postpartum mares have good appetites, and they frequently will begin eating within the first hour after foaling. Laxative feeds, such as bran-based mashes, should be fed for the first few days postpartum as well as good quality hay in moderation and pasture when available. Many people think it is a good idea to worm the mare with Ivermectin™ or Strongid™ in the first 12 to 72 hours after foaling because it can help lesson the severity of the foal heat diarrhea experienced by the foal. This idea is controversial, but if the mare has not been on a regular deworming program, she should be dewormed as soon as possible after foaling under a veterinarian's direction, then placed on a regular deworming schedule. Likewise, if the mare's vaccination history is unknown, she should receive Tetanus prophylaxis (both tetanus antitoxin and tetanus toxoid) as soon as possible after foaling.

AT A GLANCE

- Normal post-foaling mares are alert and responsive.

- Foals should nurse within one to three hours of birth.

- Colostrum intake is necessary for foals to receive antibodies from their mothers.

- Inexperienced, painful mares can show aggression when their foals try to nurse.

Lastly, the mare's udder should be examined (this can be done initially while sampling the colostrum) at least twice a day to make sure she has milk, there is no mastitis, and the foal is nursing. One of the first signs that a foal is ill is that it will "go off the bag" and stop nursing. Many sick foals will continue to "comfort nurse" for short bouts and might appear still to be eating, but when the mare's udder is examined it is full of milk and distended. A normal foal will keep the mare nursed out and the udder will be somewhat slack.

MONITORING THE FOAL

Foals should be monitored closely during the first hours and days. The transition from apparently normal foal to critically ill foal can occur rapidly, and initially the signs can be subtle. A sick neonate should be identified as quickly as possible. Many of the conditions that can afflict the very young foal are life-threatening. They include septicemia, "joint ill," umbilical abscesses, pneumonia, neonatal isoerythrolysis (anemia and jaundice due to blood type incompatibility between foal and dam), meconium impaction, and ruptured bladder. Any of these conditions require immediate veterinary intervention.

Normal foals are aware and alert within a few minutes of

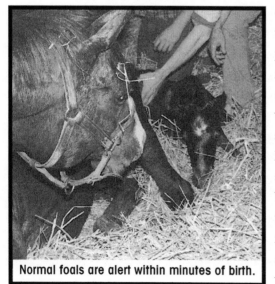

Normal foals are alert within minutes of birth.

delivery and will right themselves into a sternal position quickly. They make vigorous attempts to stand, and usually succeed within one to two hours after birth. Normal foals have an almost immediate suckle reflex and will begin seeking to nurse (on their foot, their mother's muzzle) even before they stand. Once up, the foal will search for the udder.

Often they have to make several attempts (sometimes napping in between) before succeeding. Normal foals will nurse successfully within one to three hours of delivery. They will nurse frequently and nap and even play in between. They are curious and bright and a delight to watch.

A number of management practices need to be performed to ensure that the foal gets off to a healthy start. Initially, the most important thing to ensure is that the foal's head is free of the amnion and that it is breathing. If the foal has not ruptured the white amnion during delivery, it needs to be torn open manually so the foal does not suffocate. (Again, attendants should remain calm and assist quietly and competently). If the foal is not breathing, blunt stimulation with a fingertip or piece of straw applied to the inside of the nostril is often noxious enough to cause the foal to sneeze and take a breath. The nose should be stripped of fluids by stroking down the length of the nose on either side. Rubbing the foal vigorously along its ribs also can stimulate breathing. If needed, Dopram™ (a respiratory stimulant provided at the veterinarian's discretion) can be given under the foal's tongue, and nose-to-mouth resuscitation can be initiated until the veterinarian arrives and administers more invasive resuscitation techniques. On large farms that foal many mares, a veterinarian can instruct attendants on how to provide oxygen to a newborn in critical condition, and an oxygen tank can be maintained on hand in case of an emergency.

Once it is clear that the foal is breathing and making the rapid adjustment to life outside the womb, the foal and mare should be left alone so they can rest and get acquainted. Once the umbilical cord has ruptured (usually when the mare stands or if the foal struggles), the attendant should quietly enter and dip the foal's exposed umbilicus with either a 2% tincture of iodine solution or a 0.5% chlorhexidine diacetate solution. The exposed end of the umbilicus is one of the primary entry routes for infection, so good navel care is essential. Navel infections can lead to a patent urachus, umbilical abscesses, umbilical hernias, bladder infections, blood born systemic bacterial infections (septicemia), etc.

The navel should be monitored daily to make sure it is dry and free of infection, and it should be redipped within 12 hours after birth and thereafter as needed. An umbilical cord remnant that fails to dry, is discharging pus, or seems inflamed or thickened requires veterinary examination. It is not unusual for colts to urinate on the remnant of the umbilical cord, especially a long one. In these cases, the cord will be wet with urine, but it will not be open (as in a patent urachus). When the colt urinates, there will be only one stream of urine originating from the penis. If there is a patent urachus, the foal will produce a dribble or stream of urine through its umbilicus as well as from its penis (if it is a colt) or from its vulva (if it is a filly).

Occasionally the umbilical cord does not break. Usually this occurs when the placenta detaches before the mare stands, so there is no tension left on the cord. In this event, the cord must be ruptured by the attendant. Do not cut the cord. There is a natural point in the umbilical cord about two inches from the foal's abdominal wall where it narrows and is designed to break. Making sure your hands are clean, place one hand against the foal's abdominal wall, holding the cord between the fingers. Place the other hand around the length of cord, about 12 or more inches down the cord away from the foal's body wall. (You might need to wrap the cord around that hand to maintain a secure grip.) Brace your hand so that is against the foal's abdomen and grip the cord with your fingers so that tension is applied only to the umbilical cord. Then apply steady tension and pull with the hand that is wrapped around the placental length of cord until the cord ruptures at its natural point.

Dip the cord with the disinfectant. There will be little to no bleeding because tension will cause the blood vessels to spasm and close. Cutting the cord does not cause the vessels to close, so the foal is likely to bleed more and become more susceptible to bacteria. Once the umbilicus has been cared for, the attendant should leave the stall to watch..

COLOSTRUM INTAKE

The next major hurdle is to make sure the foal nurses and therefore ingests the all-important colostrum. Failure to ingest adequate colostrum results in "failure of passive transfer" of the colostral antibodies and leaves the foal susceptible to infection. If the foal fails to nurse by three hours, the mare should be milked and the foal fed 250 to 500 ml of colostrum either via a bottle with a lamb's nipple or via stomach tube (by a veterinarian).

The foal's initial nursing attempts might appear misguided as it tries to nurse on everything except its mother's teat. The mare frequently will try to assist the foal by positioning herself and the foal so as to give it easy access to her udder, and by encouraging the foal by nuzzling its tail and buttocks. Some foals latch right on without a hitch, and others need a little time to become hungry enough to put in an honest effort. It is best to allow the foal to find the teat

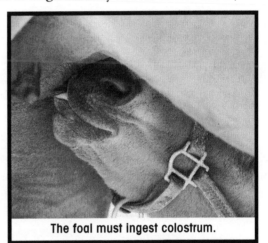

The foal must ingest colostrum.

on its own if it can, but occasionally some individuals require a little help to succeed.

When assisting, remember to move slowly and carefully when handling the mare. She can be very protective and could hurt someone if she feels the foal is threatened. This is usually a two-person job: one to hold the mare in position and one to direct the foal. The person on the mare should have a shank on her halter and should use the lightest restraint possible to get her to stand still. The mare often will be more relaxed about the "help" as long as no one gets between her and the foal and as long as she can see the foal and touch it with her muzzle. The person directing the foal will be most effective maneuvering it either by cradling it in their arms or by gently supporting and pushing its hindquarters so that the head is in the mare's flank. The least restraint and pressure applied to the foal the better because foals tend to resist if they are "pushed," and they easily become distracted. Occasionally placing an arm lightly under a foal's jaw to direct its muzzle upward toward the udder, if need be, can help. In general, though, once the foal is in the correct position to find the udder, the rest is up to him. Lightly rubbing the foal around the tail and on the buttock to mimic the mare's nuzzling often will encourage the foal to seek the udder a little more diligently.

Whether assisting or watching the foal try on his own, make sure the foal which appears to have found the mark and is suckling is actually on the teat. A foal can appear to be suckling from a distance and even sound like it and still only be applying a hickey to the side of the mare's udder. Once the foal has found the teat, however, it is its own reward and the foal will stay on until he is satisfied. Rarely do they forget where to find it when they are ready to go back for more.

The above description is intended for the normal foal. Obviously if a foal is weak or has a malformation that prevents it from standing (e.g., contracted tendons) and/or nursing effectively (e.g., wry muzzle) it should be promptly assisted to nurse or be manually supplemented with colostrum. Bottle feeding has the advantage of being easily administered provided the foal has a normal suckle. The drawback is that the foal is in danger of becoming imprinted on the nice person who fed it, and unwilling to go back to its unrewarding effort of seeking the mare's teat. There is also a danger that the foal accidentally will inhale (aspirate) the milk while drinking from a bottle. The main advantages to tube feeding are that, when properly done by a veterinarian, it ensures that the colostrum is delivered to the stomach and it is an obnoxious enough procedure that, although full, the foal is happy to return to its dam. The foal which has received good quality colostrum by three hours and continues to nurse regularly for the first 24 hours should be well protected. The end of the foal's ability to transfer antibodies from the ingested colostrum to its bloodstream is termed "gut closure." Gut closure begins within hours after birth and is complete in 24 hours.

If the colostral immunoglobulin content is poor, the foal will not be well protected, no matter how much it nurses. A calibrated equine colostrometer can estimate the immunoglobulin content of colostrum by measuring its specific gravity. Studies have shown that a colostral specific gravity of 1.060 or higher is desirable. Foals which have consumed colostrum that has a specific gravity of 1.060 or greater within the first hour after birth have been shown to have serum IgG levels that are greater than 400 mg/dL at 24 hours of age. Foals who have serum IgG levels of 800 mg/dL or greater are considered to have adequate transfer of antibodies. Foals who have serum IgG levels of 400 mg/dL or less at 24 hours of age have failure of passive transfer and risk becoming sick from inadequate immunity. Therefore, measuring the specific gravity of the mare's colostrum at foaling immediately identifies foals which will need supplementation.

A sample of colostrum is readily obtained by quietly stripping a small amount (one-quarter of a cup or less) from the mare's teat. It frequently is easiest to milk the mare into a wide-mouthed cup by standing on one side of her while the foal is nursing or seeking the udder on the other side. It also is more comfortable to the mare if the teat is lubricated with saliva or sterile lubricant applied by the fingers.

Foals should have a complete physical and have their blood drawn and tested by a veterinarian for IgG content at eight to 24 hours of age. Foals already greater than 800 mg/dL at eight to 12 hours are protected. Foals less than 800 mg/dL at eight to 12 hours can still be supplemented orally with banked colostrum as gut closure has not yet occurred. These foals should have their blood redrawn and IgG content re-evaluated at 24 hours to ensure adequate supplementation.

Foals with failure of passive transfer of maternal antibodies at 24 or more hours of age can no longer absorb antibodies orally and will require an intravenous plasma transfusion. If at all possible, a blood-typed, universal plasma donor should come from the horses that reside on the farm where the foal is born so the plasma will contain antibodies against the local disease pathogens. Though excellent products exist, commercially available plasma is produced to contain antibodies against the more common equine pathogens, but might not protect against all the organisms the foal might encounter.

Banking colostrum is a good management practice and should be performed regularly on all farms (regardless of their size) so that a good supply is available if needed. Many veterinarians maintain a banked supply; so might neighboring farms. It could be difficult, however, to find colostrum at 3 a.m. if these sources do not exist. Colostrum harvested for banking should have a minimum specific gravity of 1.060. It should come from mares free of isoantibodies against the major equine blood types to prevent Neonatal Isoerythrolysis in a supplemented foal.

(Neonatal Isoerythrolysis is a potentially fatal condition in newborn foals in which the foal's red blood cells are destroyed by antibodies absorbed from a sensitized mare's colostrum. This occurs when the foal's blood type is incompatible with the mare's. The mare has been sensitized against that blood type so that her immune system generates antibodies against foreign proteins in the foal's red blood cells. (Similar to RH Incompatibility in humans.) These antibodies are concentrated, like all other antibodies, in the colostrum. As the foal nurses, then absorbs these antibodies, they begin to break down the red blood cells. The more colostrum the foal has ingested, the greater the destruction of the cells. The foal becomes jaundiced, anemic, and progressively weaker. Death can occur in as little as 24 hours if the condition is not identified and the foal not treated with blood transfusions.)

Mares can be tested for isoantibodies one month before foaling, or the compatibility between the foal's blood and the mare's blood can be tested at birth before the foal nurses. Should an incompatibility exist, the foal should not be permitted to nurse the mare for the first 24 hours (the foal should be muzzled). The foal will require supplemental colostrum from an alternative safe source. Sensitization of mares usually occurs over multiple pregnancies, making the condition uncommon in maiden mares. Mares which have had one jaundiced foal likely will have others, and it is prudent to test these mares against the siring stallion's blood type on each subsequent pregnancy. All of her foalings must be attended so that an at-risk foal does not nurse from the mare.

Mares donating colostrum can provide 250 ml of colostrum once their foals have nursed for the first time. This small amount will not "rob" the mare's own foal of any immunity or nutrition. The collected colostrum should be strained through gauze or cheesecloth to remove any dirt, hair, or other debris, then placed into a clean container. The container should be clearly labeled with the donor mare's name, the date it was harvested, and the specific gravity of the colostrum. The colostrum is then frozen and stored in a standard freezer, where it can be maintained in good condition for 12 to 18 months. When needed, the colostrum should be thawed slowly in warm water. Care must be taken not to overheat the colostrum while thawing because "cooking" will destroy the antibodies. It is a good practice to replenish the colostrum supply as each eligible donor has a foal, and to discard any old, unused colostrum as it becomes outdated.

Lastly, the newborn foal should be observed closely during the first few hours after birth to be sure that it passes its meconium (first feces). The meconium is typically a dark fecal material that has accumulated in the foal's intestines during gestation, and the foal typically passes it during the first four hours of life. The amount can be quite large, and most foals will begin passing multiple piles after they have nursed for the first time. This fecal material can be firm and well-formed into dense "nuggets." Usually the foal will concentrate, lift its tail, and strain to pass it. As the material is cleared from the rectum, the consistency becomes softer and more pasty.

The concern is that sometimes there is quite a bit of material and it can be very hard. When this occurs the foal can become impacted and colic just the same as any older horse with a blocked intestine. In an effort to prevent an impaction and facilitate passage of the meconium, enemas commonly are administered to foals after birth. I prefer to wait until after the foal has nursed before administering the enema to avoid interrupting the mare-foal bonding process and distracting the foal from nursing. Occasionally a foal will start to strain before nursing. In these instances we will administer the enema sooner. A human enema bottle, or soft rubber feeding tube and siphon, can be used to administer 60 to 120 ml of warm, soapy water repeatedly as needed to the foal's rectum. The foal typically will begin straining and pass fecal material within a few minutes.

A veterinarian or knowledgeable, experienced attendant should administer the enema, because if done improperly it can damage the foal's rectum. Even after the foal has passed some fecal material, it should be observed carefully over the first 24 hours for signs of straining as the meconium could be voluminous and the foal still could become impacted. Should continued straining or signs of colic be noted, call a veterinarian at once. Medical management of meconium impactions includes repeat enemas, administering laxatives such as mineral oil via a naso-gastric tube, and hydrating with IV fluids. If an impaction persists, gas will begin to build up in the intestine behind the blockage, causing pain. The foal likely will stop nursing and begin displaying signs of colic. Unresponsive impactions will require surgical intervention.

The veterinarian will examine the foal's GI function closely during the first physical, as well as observe its appetite and demeanor. The first physical exam is performed at eight to 24 hours of age when blood is drawn to measure the foal's IgG levels. Vitals (temperature, pulse, and respiratory rate) are measured to make sure they are normal. The umbilicus is examined carefully for wetness, heat, swelling, or discharge. The foal's joints are palpated for signs of heat or swelling. The legs are assessed for contracture or angular limb deformities. The mouth is examined to make sure the foal doesn't have a cleft palate, and the gums

Examining the new foal.

are checked to make sure they are a healthy pink and not jaundiced, red, or pale. Next the eyes are examined for cataracts and signs of septicemia (presence of inflammation in the anterior chamber of the eye or increased prominence of the blood vessels in the sclera). The chest is auscultated to make sure the heart and lungs sound normal, and the ribs are palpated to make sure none fractured during foaling. The abdomen is also auscultated to make sure the foal has normal gut sounds, and the mare's udder is checked to make sure the foal is nursing.

The veterinarian likely will ask the owner if the foal has urinated and whether it has been straining. Blood will be drawn for an IgG and possibly also for a complete blood count (CBC) if indicated. If the foal lives in a selenium-deficient area it might get a vitamin E and selenium injection as a protection against White Muscle Disease. If there is any question about the tetanus vaccination status of the mare, the foal also will be given tetanus antitoxin and toxoid shots.

Remember, it is important to bring any concerns or abnormalities to the veterinarian's attention as soon as they are noted. Fortunately, most foals are born healthy and good management helps them to stay that way.

THE BONDING PROCESS AND FOAL REJECTION

Foal rejection rarely occurs in horses. Complete rejection of the foal by its dam occurs in only about 1% of the foaling population. Maiden mares and/or mares with dystocia are the most likely and common candidates. Mares from certain family lines of Arabian horses also show a possible genetic predisposition for repeated aggression toward successive foals. Normally, the mare's maternal instinct is an amazing thing. Mares form exceptionally strong bonds with their neonatal foals within the first few hours after birth and can be

Mares instinctively protect their foals.

quite protective. It is thought that mares recognize their foals primarily through smell and taste. This recognition forms during birth (when the placental membranes have ruptured and the mare initially smells the allantoic fluids) and after birth as the mare licks and nuzzles the wet foal.

The young foal is most vulnerable when lying down. They are deep sleepers and also have some difficulty (compared to other species) rising quickly to their feet. Because of this, mares normally are especially protective of their foals when the foal is recumbent. During the first few days, foals also are inclined to follow any large moving object and seem to take some time learning to recognize and follow their dams. As a result, most mares tend to keep themselves between their foals and any perceived threat and to warn other horses (and people) away from their foals, in part, so the foal does not become confused and follow someone other than her. Mares also initiate frequent "walk aways" from their nursing foals so the foals have to follow the mares. It is assumed this is how the foal learns to stay close to the mare and recognize her as its sole source of food and safety.

Mares are rarely aggressive toward their foals. When they do display aggression, it almost always occurs in association with the foal's nursing. The suckling act itself appears to be pleasing to the mare, and it is thought that she gains relief when a full udder is nursed dry. By contrast, the nuzzling and bumping of the udder by the newborn seeking it for the first time and later on by the hungry youngster trying to get his mother to let down her milk is probably uncomfortable and even painful to the mare whose udder is tense and engorged with milk and edema.

Observe a mare nursing her foal. As the foal initially seeks and bumps, the mare often will grimace and pin her ears. If the foal is particularly rough, she might even turn her head and bite the foal on its rump. As the foal settles down and begins to nurse, however, the mare's eye will soften and get a "faraway" look, her body will relax, and frequently she will relax the hind leg opposite to the side the foal is nursing on. The association between relief from an engorged udder and the foal nursing is something the mare must learn.

The majority of maiden mares which "reject" are actually rejecting the nursing process rather than the foal itself. The initial attempts at nursing hurt and frighten these mares. They do not want to stand still, and could progress to kicking and biting at the foal as it attempts to find the udder. By contrast, experienced mares frequently do everything they can to encourage the foal to nurse for the first time (position their bodies to facilitate proper positioning by the foal, pushing and nuzzling the foal into position, standing stock still, etc.). They appear almost to "grin and bear" the foal's initial pokes and jabs, then sigh in relief as the foal finally latches onto the teat and nurses. On the other hand, mares which have had a painful dystocia or are experiencing pain in the initial post-partum period (strong stage III uterine contractions, for example) appear to associate the presence of the foal with causing the pain and reject its advances. Some even try to drive the foal away.

When a newborn foal requires human intervention and assistance to survive, the initial bonding process could be disturbed and the mare (especially a first-time mother) prevented from recognizing that she has a foal. Excited and overzealous foaling attendants also can interfere with the bonding process. This can happen if they rush in to dry a foal, changing its smell, and make a big fuss over it and exclude the dam. Human helpers also inadvertently can increase a mare's tension and fear during the initial nursing period by trying to rush events, confusing a maiden mare, and causing her ultimately to reject her foal. Attendants should enter the stall only when necessary. Before foaling, it is good to accustom the maiden mare to having her udder handled so when the foal starts to nurse the sensation is not completely new.

In some instances, a mare demonstrates motherly concern for her foal (i.e., licks and nickers to the foal and acts protectively), but will not permit the foal to nurse. Quietly restraining the mare by holding her halter and reassuring her with words and touch as the foal tries to nurse sometimes can solve this problem. Punishment is usually counterproductive as most of these mares are frightened and rough handling only makes them more so. As soon as the mare relaxes and stands still, she should be praised. If she wants to turn her head and touch the foal and nuzzle its hindquarters, allow her to do so. It sometimes helps to milk the mare by hand initially to alleviate udder soreness. (In this instance, it is a good idea to feed the foal this stripped colostrum either by bottle or via naso-gastric tube.) Once the pain is gone, most maiden mares are more willing to permit the foal to nurse.

Some mares which strongly resist nursing might require sedation or twitching. Acepromazine seems to work especially well in this instance, perhaps because it promotes prolactin release in addition to having a calming effect. In situations in which the mare is particularly resistant and/or behaves aggressively toward the foal (biting and kicking) it might become necessary to place her behind a restraining bar so the foal can nurse safely without being kicked or pinned against the bar or wall. The mare's head also should be restrained so she cannot bite the foal, and she should not be left unattended. The foal is given the rest of the box stall in which to move about freely. In this manner, the mare is forced to allow the foal to nurse, and has constant exposure to the foal so she cannot forget about it. In time (within a few days to a few weeks) many resistant mares will accept the foal. Foals whose mothers absolutely refuse to accept them should be removed for their own safety and either hand reared or (preferably) placed with a willing nurse mare.

Mares whose foals require intensive care in the early postpartum period should be permitted to remain in as close contact with the foal as possible. If the foal is unable to nurse, the mare should be milked every one to two hours to keep her lactating with the hope that the foal will recover.

Mares which are inattentive or resistant because of pain from sources other than the udder should first be examined to make sure the cause is nothing serious, then treated at the veterinarian's discretion with analgesics (low dose Banamine) and/or hand walking to relieve the pain. Once the pain is gone, most mares are eager to bond with their babies.

In all instances, remember to place the safety of the handlers first. A frightened, hurting mare can pose a danger. Also, many mares which reject nursing are still protective of their offspring and might resent anyone coming between them and their foals, sometimes becoming frantic if an attempt is made to remove the foal. Only experienced handlers should restrain these mares. Fortunately, most maiden mares which successfully bond with their first foal do not repeat these behaviors at subsequent foalings.

CHAPTER 10

Post-Foaling Management of the Mare

The mare has an amazing capacity to recover rapidly from foaling. Barring any complications or metritis, the mare returns to a fertile estrous period within five to 12 days, on average, and the first ovulation typically occurs eight to 12 days after parturition. As always, some mares might ovulate sooner than eight days and others will go longer than 12, and in general mares ovulate sooner relative to foaling if they foal later in the spring (closer to the physiological breeding season) as compared with earlier foaling mares.

In order to conceive on this "foal heat" and go on to establish and maintain a new pregnancy, the mare's postpartum uterus must return rapidly to its pre-pregnancy size and condition. During this post-foaling period, the uterus actively contracts almost continuously. This causes the uterus to shrink rapidly and helps it to clear the normal fluid, lochia, and bacterial contamination present after foaling. The normally involuting uterus will shrink back into the mare's pelvis within about 10 days of foaling, and it will return completely to its pre-pregnancy size by 30 days.

Likewise, the uterine lining needs to make the transition from pregnant to non-pregnant state to be ready to support a new embryo. If uterine involution is normal (and the mare has not experienced any complications), the endometrium usually will be completely regenerated by 14 days after foaling. When conditions are right, therefore, it is possible for a mare to foal, return to estrus, be re-bred, and establish a new pregnancy within two weeks of the birth of her foal.

The normal foaling event itself can generate quite a bit of bacterial uterine contamination. The cervix is wide open in the immediate post-foaling period, the vagina, vestibule, and vulva have been greatly stretched open, and it is very easy for bacteria to gain access into the uterus. Cultures taken from the uterus during the postpartum/foal heat periods

---

AT A GLANCE

• Mares can go into heat five to 12 days after foaling.

• Mares should receive a complete examination seven days after foaling.

• Foal heat breeding can help mares foal in a timely manner year to year.

• Limit grain and keep newly weaned mares under supervision at pasture to help with the "drying off" of their milk supply.

---

invariably will be positive for a mix of contaminating organisms. One of the functions of the foal heat is to help the mare clear this bacterial contamination so she does not become persistently infected and develop a postpartum endometritis. Anything that interferes with and delays normal uterine involution (retained placenta, decreased uterine fluid clearance, foaling injuries that lead to chronic contamination) puts the mare at risk for developing an infection and damaging her reproductive capabilities. Management of the mare in the immediate postpartum period, therefore, is aimed at preventing problems and rapidly identifying abnormalities in order to correct them.

It is important that the mare get adequate exercise in the form of turnout in a paddock (weather permitting) or a clean arena with her young foal during the first days after foaling. Hand walking is also a good alternative if the mare tends to be silly when she is initially turned out with her young foal and endangers it by running excessively. Walking helps the mare's abdominal and pelvic tissues regain muscle tone and helps the uterus clear fluid. Confined mares, such as those whose foals are ill, are at risk of pooling excessive amounts of uterine fluid, which creates an inviting environment for bacteria. The mare's attitude should be monitored to make sure she is bright, eating, and interested in and caring for her foal. Mares which appear dull and depressed and/or develop a fever need to be examined by a veterinarian.

The quantity and character of the mare's vulvar discharge also should be monitored closely. Frank blood or pus are immediate cause for concern and veterinary examination. Normally a mare's discharge will appear serous and slightly bloody in the first few hours after foaling, then become more amber colored and mucoid. It should appear mucoid and clear within a week. At no point should the discharge become excessive, and it is a good idea to examine the underside of the mare's tail and the tail hairs for accumulated debris.

The mare's perineum should be cleaned once or twice daily with a mild soap and rinsed clean with water as needed. Cleansing decreases the likelihood of accumulated discharge causing skin irritation in the perineal region or the mare picking up a uterine infection because of the increased

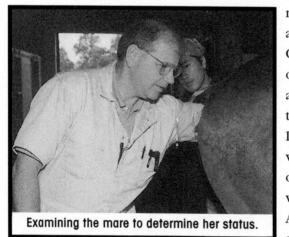

Examining the mare to determine her status.

number of bacteria around her vulva. Cleaning also allows the observer to assess more accurately the amount the mare is discharging. Discharge that remains watery, copious, or blood or pus-tinged warrants veterinary attention. Application of ointment such as Preparation H™ to the outside skin of the perineum and vulva also might help reduce swelling in this region in mares which are excessively bruised and swollen.

Unless a problem exists, the mare's first thorough reproductive examination should be performed seven days after foaling. At this time, the cervix has had a chance to begin closing from its dilated state, making it harder for air to enter the uterus during a vaginal speculum examination. Also, the mare should be returning to her "foal heat" and estimations of when she might ovulate can begin to be made.

This examination includes: 1) An overall assessment of the mare's attitude and condition; 2) Visual and tactile examination of the mare's perineum to assess the amount of damage done at foaling and the degree of tissue healing up to that point; 3) A rectal palpation and ultrasound to assess the degree of uterine involution (tone and size of the uterus and quantity and quality of any inter-uterine fluid that might be present) and also to identify what structures might be on the ovary (i.e., Are the ovaries active? Is there a dominant follicle present yet, and what size is it? Has she already had a post-foaling ovulation and now there is a CH or CL present on the ovary?); 4) A vaginal speculum examination to assess the vestibule, vagina, and cervix for bruising or tears, and to assess whether the mare is pooling any urine or exudate in her vagina. It is not uncommon for a mare to be pooling a small amount of urine in her vagina at this time, and in many cases the pooling will resolve once the pelvic tissues have tightened back up; and 5) A digital vaginal examination to feel for any tears in the vagina and especially the cervix. Many cervical tears can be detected only by feeling the external cervical os and the cervical lumen and internal os directly with a sterile, gloved hand.

Mares which are free of injury and involuting normally, have little to no accumulations of vaginal or uterine fluid, and who have not ovulated at this point are potential candidates for foal heat breeding. Most mares which are not foal heat breeding candidates will be recovered and ready to be bred by their "30-day heat" (the first ovulation, plus 21 days). Some of these mares might even be short cycled from their foal heat ovulation with prostaglandin and bred sooner.

Breeding on the foal heat can be controversial. Conception rates from foal heat breedings can be as much as 10% to 20% lower than those seen breeding later post foaling cycles, and there is some question as to whether there is an increased incidence of early embryonic loss associated with these pregnancies. The lower success rates arise, of course, from attempting to breed mares which have delayed involution, post-foaling metritis, and/or unhealed foaling injuries. All these factors will decrease fertility. When foal heat breeding candidates are chosen based on a strict set of criteria, the pregnancy rates can be comparable to those seen in mares bred at later cycles.

A foal heat candidate needs to have foaled uneventfully (no dystocia and no retained placenta). At seven days after foaling the mare must not have bruising or tearing in her vagina or cervix, have nothing worse than a mild first-degree perineal laceration, be involuting normally, have no excessive accumulations of uterine fluid, and have no evidence of exudate or urine pooling in her vagina.

Lastly, a good candidate for foal heat breeding should ovulate for the first time 10 or more days after foaling. As previously mentioned, it normally takes the uterine lining 14 days to regenerate and be ready to support and maintain a new embryo. The embryo does not reach the uterus until five to six days after ovulation (it is in the oviduct up until this time). Therefore, breeding only those mares which ovulate 10 or more days after foaling ensures that the endometrium will be ready to support a pregnancy by the time the new embryo reaches the uterus (i.e., at day 15-plus post foaling), and therefore decreases the likelihood of early embryonic loss.

The main advantage to achieving a pregnancy on a foal heat is to enable the mare to foal earlier the following season. In those breeds where a January, February, or March foal is preferred over a foal born later in the season, it is important to have the mare pregnant again by April. Successfully establishing a pregnancy on the foal heat means the mare will foal one month earlier the next season (i.e., if she foaled in May this year and becomes pregnant on the foal heat, she will foal sometime in April of the next year). When managed correctly, foal heat breeding is a useful tool for helping mares to continue to foal in a timely manner from year to year, and provides a means for "backing up" a late foaling mare so she does not have to be left open for a year. It is important to remember, however, that only those mares meeting the criteria should be bred on foal heats. It will save time in the long run to wait to breed less than ideal candidates because the chance for success will increase when the mare is at her optimum condition.

WEANING CONCERNS FOR THE BROODMARE

Most foals are weaned when they are about six months old (four to nine months seems to be the most common age range). Whether the foals are weaned isolated in their stalls or are kept in a safely fenced pasture in familiar surroundings with their established group of horses (mares and foals they have known all their lives), the management of the removed mares should be the same. In my experience, pasture weaning seems to be the least stressful for the weanling. But when weaning in this manner, make sure to leave with the group only tolerant mares which will accept the role of baby-sitter.

Weaned mares should be led quickly and quietly onto a waiting van (sedation can be given if needed), and transported away from their foals to where they can no longer hear the foal calling or see where they were both previously housed. She will quickly accept the "loss" of her foal (usually within a couple of hours or a day) and settle into her new surroundings. It helps to place the mare in a "remote," safely fenced pasture with one or two other established, calm, sociable adult mares so she will be reassured by their presence and occupied with becoming part of the group.

Ideally, the newly weaned mare is kept at pasture. The constant walking about to graze and drink helps to minimize swelling and edema in the engorged udder, and hastens its involution ("drying off"). Cessation of milk production by the cells of the mammary gland is caused by the back pressure of congested, unnursed milk in the mammary alveoli. Removing milk from the udder keeps the intermammary pressures low and keeps milk production going. It therefore is counterproductive, and in the long run harder on the mare, to remove milk from the engorged udder because it prolongs the drying off process. Anti-inflammatories can help relieve the mare's discomfort if it is extreme, but unless she has developed mastitis the gland should not be stripped out.

Most foals are weaned by six months.

Discontinuing the mare's grain ration, and limiting her to grass pasture and hay (for one to three weeks, and even longer if the mare does not require grain) further will help her to cease milk production by removing the extra dietary energy and protein the grain provides. In instances where the mare and foal pairs are fed individually in their stalls and not as part of a group, the mare's grain ration can be decreased over the few days before the actual weaning before its complete withdrawal.

In no circumstances should the weaned mare's water supply be limited. Dehydration will hasten the drying off process, but it also will predispose the mare to impaction colic, especially when combined with stress and abrupt diet change. Remember, too, that many mares will be pregnant at the time of weaning and so stress and dehydration need to be kept at a minimum.

During the drying-off period, it is also important to check the mare's gland daily (two to three times if possible) for signs of mastitis, and notify a veterinarian if a problem is detected. The average mare's udder will be shrinking within five days, and will be back to pre-pregnancy size within a month. Mares which have just weaned their first foal will not return completely to their maiden mare appearance. Typically, the teats will be larger than before she nursed a foal and the gland halves will remain somewhat prominent but slack and shrunken back up into her groin. In other words, she will have the appearance of the mother she has become.

Abdomen — Area of the body between the chest and the pelvis containing the viscera; also called the belly.

Abdominocentesis — Puncturing the abdominal wall in order to collect peritoneal fluid or to facilitate drainage.

Abdominal press — Active, "voluntary" contraction of, and pushing with, the abdominal muscles.

Abortion — Expulsion of a fetus between 50 and 300 days of gestation.

Abortion storm — The loss of multiple fetuses from multiple mares during a narrow time frame on a single farm or geographic area.

Accessory sex glands — The seminal vesicles, prostate, and bulbo urethral glands of the stallion.

Adrenal corticosteroids — Hormones produced by the adrenal cortex (e.g., cortisol), frequently in response to stress.

Aerosol transmission — The spread of an agent from one individual to another via vapor droplets that are exhaled by one animal and inhaled by another.

Agalactia — Failure to produce milk postpartum.

Allantochorion/Chorioallantois — The fused chorionic and allantoic placental membranes.

Allantoic cavity — The fluid-filled placental cavity between the allantochorion and the amnionic placental membranes.

Allantoic fluid — The fluid that fills the allantoic cavity. This fluid acts as a protective cushion around the fetus.

Allantois — The placental membrane that contains the fetal/placental vasculature.

Altrenogest — Synthetic progesterone (Regu-Mate ™).

Amnion — White placental membrane that immediately surrounds the fetus.

Amnionic cavity — The fluid-filled, placental space or cavity between the developing foal and the amnionic membrane.

Anemic — Blood condition in which the concentration of hemoglobin (and frequently the concentration of red blood cells as well) is below normal levels.

Angel slippers — Membranous pads which cover the unborn foal's hooves and serve to protect the soft tissues of the mare's reproductive tract from the foal's hoof edges during development and during delivery.

Anterior chamber — The fluid-filled "front" chamber of the eye, between the cornea and the iris.

Anthelminitics — Compounds which kill and/or cause the expulsion of intestinal parasites.

Artificial insemination — Replacing the normal copulatory act between two animals by manually collecting semen from the stallion, then placing it (usually transvaginally) directly into the mare's uterus.

Ascending infection — An infection that spreads "upward or inward" from one body structure into another (i.e., from the vagina, through the cervix, and into the uterus).

Aseptic — Free of contamination.

Auscult — Listen to the chest or abdomen, usually with a stethoscope.

Avillous — Lacking villi.

Bacteremia — The presence of live bacteria loose in the blood stream.

Barren mare — A mare who has failed to establish a viable pregnancy after having been bred during the previous breeding season and who is now not pregnant.

Blastocyst — Stage of embryonic development during which the developing embryo is a hollow sphere of cells.

Breeding season — The natural equine breeding season occurs during the spring and summer when day length is long. In response to increasing day length mares begin to cycle. Mares are referred to as seasonally polyestrus, long day breeders.

Broad ligaments — Sheets of supportive connective tissue that form the reproductive mesentery that suspends the mare's uterus, oviducts, and ovaries from the pelvis.

Broad spectrum antibiotics — An antibiotic or combination of antibiotics that is effective against a number of different types of bacterial organisms.

Capsule — A glycoprotein coat that surrounds the developing equine embryo from approximately day 8 to day 19 of gestation.

Caslick's — Procedure in which the edges of the vulvar lips are surgically cut, then sewn together from the top of the vulva to part way down its length so that the vulvar lips will heal together to form a protective barrier between the outside air and contaminants and the interior structures of the mare's reproductive tract. As the vulva is not sewn completely closed, discharge and urine are still free to pass outwards. This procedure is indicated in mares whose vulvar and perineal conformation predisposes them to developing pneumovagina, and is a surgical correction of a conformational defect that could contribute to infertility in a mare.

Cervical star — A normally avillous area on the chorionic surface of the placenta that corresponds to where the chorion was adjacent to the internal os of the cervix.

Cervix — In the mare the cervix is a narrow tubo-muscular structure that connects the vaginal and uterine lumens. It is composed of an external vaginal opening (external os), a straight tubular body, and an internal uterine opening (internal os). During diestrus and especially during pregnancy the cervix is tightly closed to prevent outside contamination and invading organisms from gaining access to the uterine lumen.

Cesarean section — Surgical delivery of a foal across the uterine and abdominal walls.

Conception — The successful fertilization of the mare's oocyte with a stallion's spermatozoa to form a new individual.

Chorion — The red, velvety appearing placental membrane that directly attaches to the mare's uterus via thousands of interlocking/ interdigitating microvilli in order to facilitate nutrient, waste, and oxygen exchange between the fetal and maternal blood circulations.

Chorionic girdle — "Equatorial region" on the trophoblastic layer of the developing embryo from which the cells that form the endometrial cups originate.

Cleft palate — Developmental defect in which either the soft or hard palate (or both) are not completely closed, thereby forming a communication between the normally separate nasal and oral cavities.

Colic — Abdominal pain.

Colitis — Inflammation of the colon, frequently resulting in diarrhea.

Colostrum — The first milk produced by the mare at foaling which is rich in protective antibodies the foal needs to ingest as soon as possible during the first 24 hours of its life in order to receive the humoral immunity that will protect it for the first few months until its own immune system reaches competency.

Contracted tendons — Usually manifested as a flexural deformity seen in the newborn and sometimes fast-growing foals in which the rate of elongation of the limb bones exceeds the rate of elongation in the flexor tendons, resulting in a relative contracture of the limb in a flexed position.

Corpus hemorrhagicum — Blood-filled, ovarian structure that forms in the collapsed follicle immediately post ovulation. This structure then goes on to organize and develop into the corpus luteum.

Corpus luteum — Ovarian structure that forms post ovulation from the cells that previously lined the ovulated follicle. The corpus luteum produces progesterone.

Culture — The propagation of microorganisms in a nutrient medium. Used loosely to also describe the act of sampling the mare's uterus in order to then culture the gathered specimen to check for microorganisms.

Cycling — Refers to a mare who is undergoing the normal transitions through the estrous cycle (proestrus-estrus-metestrus-diestrus) and is ovulating in association with her estrus periods.

Decomposition — Organic decay or disintegration.

Devitalized — Dead.

Diestrus — Period of the mare's estrous cycle which is characterized by the presence of a corpus luteum on the ovary, lack of receptivity to the stallion, and production of the hormone progesterone.

Diestrus ovulation — An ovulation which occurs during the mid to late diestrus period as opposed to during the normal estrus period of the mare's cycle. Because there is an active corpus luteum already present on the ovary that is secreting progesterone at the same time that this unusual ovulation is occurring, the mare remains unreceptive to a teaser. The diestrus ovulation can be a fertile ovulation.

Double ovulation — Two ovulations that occur within the same estrus period.

Dummy foal — Term referring to a foal suffering from neonatal maladjustment syndrome. Affected foals can have a poor suckling reflex, be disoriented, and even have seizures. Frequently these foal's also are septicemic due to failure of passive transfer. Dummy foals are believed to have been oxygen deprived during the birthing process. These foals also are sometimes referred to as "Barker foals" as many of them vocalize with a "barking" sound rather than a normal whinny.

Dysmature — Foal born small, thin, and premature in appearance, but after a longer than average gestational length (i.e. more than 350 days).

Dystocia — Difficult delivery of a foal.

Early embryonic loss — Failure of an equine embryo to develop and survive past the first 30-plus days of gestation.

Edema — Swelling of any part of the body due to collection of fluid in the intercellular spaces of the tissues.

Edematous — Full of edema.

Electrolyte — Any substance which, when in solution, dissociates into ions, thus becoming capable of conducting an electric current.

Embryo — An organism in the earliest stage of development.

Embryonic fixation — In the horse the diameter of the equine embryo at about 17 days of gestation begins to exceed the diameter of the uterine lumen. At this point the embryo is no longer free to continue migrating throughout the uterus and becomes "fixed" in its position within the uterine lumen, usually at the base of one of the uterine horns.

Embryonic vesicle — Taken as a whole, the fluid-filled embryonic trophoblast membranes/yolk sack/developing allantois and embryo proper.

Endemic — Relating to any disease prevalent continually in a particular locality.

Endogenous — Originating within the body.

Endometrial cups — Placental structure formed at 35 to 40 days of gestation from trophoblast cells which invade the maternal endometrium to form conglomerates of fetal trophoblast cells that produce equine chorionic gonadatropin (ECG) from approximately 40 to 90-plus days of the equine gestation. ECG acts to support the primary CL and stimulate the production of secondary CLs on the ovaries of the pregnant mare. The endometrial cups have a life span independent of the viability of the pregnancy and will persist and function once formed even if the developing fetus is lost.

Endometrial cyst — Usually refers to a lymphatic cyst that forms in the endometrial lining of a mare's uterus.

Endometrium — The mucosal uterine lining.

Endometritis — Inflammation of the lining of the uterus, frequently due to either an infection or a chemical irritant.

Endotoxin — A toxin produced and retained by bacterial cells and released only by destruction or death of the cells.

Enema — The infusion of a fluid into the rectum for cleansing or other therapeutic purposes.

Enteritis — Inflammation of the intestines.

Epidural — Injection of an anesthetic agent upon or over the dura matter of the spinal cord in order to desensitize the perineum /pelvic region.

Equine chorionic gonadotropin — Hormone produced by the equine placenta's endometrial cups between days 40 to 90-plus of gestation.

Estrone sulfate — Conjugated estrogen produced by the live equine fetal-placental unit. Elevated levels are detectable in the pregnant mare's blood or urine reliably from 90 days until term during gestation.

Estrus — Period of the estrous cycle during which the mare is receptive to being bred by the stallion, and has an ovulatory follicle(s) present on the ovary that is producing large amounts of estrogen. Also referred to as "heat."

Exogenous — Originating outside the body.

Exsanguination — Draining the blood out of the body.

Failure of passive transfer — Failure of the newborn foal to ingest adequate amounts of good quality colostrum within the first 24 hours of life, resulting in the foal's being extremely susceptible to infection due to a lack of circulating antibodies.

Ferguson's reflex — Neuroendocrine reflex by which oxytocen release from the mare's brain is stimulated due to stretching and/or manipulation of the cervix during labor or manual manipulation .

Fertilization — The union of a spermatozoa with an oocyte.

Fetal diarrhea — Term referring to the presence of meconium (first feces) in the amnionic fluid surrounding the foal within the amnion at birth, accepted as a sign of fetal stress.

Fetal membranes — The placenta.

Fetotomy — Dismemberment of a dead (usually malformed or malpositioned) foal within the mare's uterus in order to facilitate delivery during a dystocia.

Fetus — The unborn, developing individual. In horses, this term refers to the developing foal from day 40 of gestation until term.

Fibrosis — In regard to the mare's uterus, this term refers to the formation of "scar tissue" within the endometrium.

Flehman — Characteristic, exaggerated lip curling demonstrated by horses (stallions and geldings especially) typically after sniffing urine or a mare's genitalia, but also might be seen in horses in pain.

Flushing — The process of mildly restricting caloric intake through the fall in open mares, then placing them on an increasing plane of nutrition starting in December. This coincides with placing the mares under artificial lighting to increase the mare's "day length." The addition to the mare's photoperiod stimulates her to begin cycling in advance of the normal physiological breeding season and it is thought manipulating the mare's caloric intake in this manner at the same time could further stimulate her to initiate cycling. The practice of manipulating the seasonal nature of the mare's reproductive patterns is done to meet the demands of the artificially imposed universal "birthdays" of some breed registries.

Foal heat — The first postpartum estrus which typically begins three to 10 days post foaling with the first post partum ovulation occurring typically seven to 14 days post foaling.

Follicle — Ovarian structure containing an oocyte, fluid filled in its later developmental stages. Mares generally ovulate follicles that are between 35 to 55mm in diameter. The follicle produces the steroid hormone estrogen and is the dominant ovarian structure during estrus.

Fraternal twins — Twins which arise from two different pairings of oocytes and sperm cells.

Gestation — The period of time between conception and birth.

Gravid — Pregnant.

Gut closure — Term referring to the cessation of the neonatal intestine's ability to absorb immunoglobulins (antibodies) from ingested colostrum across the intestinal wall and into the foal's bloodstream. Gut closure occurs at an increasing rate starting at birth and is complete when the foal is approximately 24 hours old.

Hand stripping — Milking or expressing milk from the mare's teat by hand.

Heat — Estrus. Period of behavioral receptivity to being bred by a stallion.

Hematoma — A localized mass of blood outside of the blood vessels, usually found in a partly clotted state.

Hemolytic anemia — An anemia caused by the disintegration of red blood cells.

Hemorrhagic — Characterized by bleeding.

Hippomane — A soft, tan mass varying in size from a few millimeters up to several centimeters in diameter and thickness that is commonly found free floating within the allantoic cavity of the equine placenta. One possible source for a nidus for this concretion of cells are the sloughed endometrial cups.

Histotroph — "Uterine milk" produced by the endometrial glands, this product is thought to nourish the developing conceptus and fetus, and be vital to pregnancy maintenance at least until the placenta has become fully established.

Histopathology — The pathology of abnormal or diseased tissue; also sometimes used to refer to the microscopic examination of diseased or abnormal tissues.

Hormone — A glandular chemical secretion produced by one organ or part of the body and carried in the bloodstream to a target organ to stimulate or retard its function.

Hydrops — Condition referring to the abnormal accumulation of placental fluid in either the allantoic (most common) or amnionic cavities.

Identical twins — Twins which result from an abnormal cleavage of one individual zygote arising from the pairing of a single oocyte and spermatazoa so that two separate individuals arise from what was initially a single cell.

Ileus — Gut stasis.

Immune compromise — Suppression of the function of the immune system.

Immunoglobulin — A protein molecule functioning as a specific antibody.

Immunoglobulin G (IgG) — The most abundant class of immunoglobulins, they provide immunity to bacteria, viruses, parasites, and fungi that have a blood-borne dissemination.

Impaction — A blockage of the intestinal lumen with ingesta, parasites, or foreign material (sand, cloth, etc.)

Implantation — The process by which the rudimentary beginnings of placentation are initiated. In the horse this does not begin to occur until approximately days 35 to 40 of gestation.

Inapparent infection — An infection which displays no outward clinical signs.

Interdigitation — Interlocking of structures by means of finger-like processes.

Interface — A surface forming a common boundary between two bodies.

Isoantibody — An antibody produced by one individual which reacts with antigens of another individual of the same species.

Jaundice — Yellow pigmentation of the skin and/or the sclera and mucous membranes caused by high levels of biliruben in the blood. Also referred to as icterus.

Joint ill — A condition, usually seen in young foals, where one or more joints becomes infected, swollen and inflamed after being seeded with a blood-borne organism (usually bacterial).

Lactation — The production of milk.

Laminitis — Inflammation of the sensitive lamina of the equine foot. Causes acute and chronic lameness, and if severe enough can result in separation of the hoof wall from the underlying structures of the foot. In extreme cases the coffin bone can rotate down through the sole of the foot or the entire hoof wall can become detached and the horse's foot "sinks" completely out of its supportive attachments. Also referred to as founder.

Larva — The worm-like, early stages in the development of certain organisms.

Live cover — Refers to the natural mating, whether at pasture or in hand, of a stallion and a mare.

Lochia — The normal blood, mucous, and cellular discharge from the uterus following labor and birth.

Loin — The part of the back between where the ribs end and the pelvis begins.

Lumen — The interior space of a tubular structure.

Luteolysis — Destruction of the corpus luteum, terminating its production of progesterone.

Maiden mare — A mare which has never had a foal; also can refer to a mare which has never been bred.

Mammary gland — The glandular tissue that produces milk.

Mastitis — Inflammation (usually due to infection) of the mammary gland.

Maternal recognition of pregnancy — Term referring to the point during pregnancy when the embryo signals the mother that it is present, thereby blocking production of prostaglandin by the uterus which would otherwise terminate the pregnancy and return the mare to estrus. In the mare this occurs on approximately day 14 post ovulation.

Meconium — The dark-colored feces produced in the intestines during fetal life and present in the rectum and colon at birth.

Medium — Substance used to cultivate the growth of bacteria.

Mesentery — A double layer of peritoneum connective tissue that attaches the various organs and viscera to the body wall and conveys to them their blood vessels and nerves.

Microcotyledons — Microscopic congregations of attachment between the uterine endometrium and the chorionic villi over the entire endometrial/placental surface area attachment.

Microvilli — Submicroscopic finger-like projections on the surface of the cell membrane which greatly increase the surface area.

Milk let down — Process by which the mare is stimulated by the presence of her foal and its suckling action to release oxytocen, which in turn acts on smooth muscle cells within the mammary gland, causing them to contract and "squeeze" milk out of the glandular tissue and on down into the duct system so that it can be suckled from the teat and ingested by the foal.

Morula — Stage during embryonic development during which the embryo is merely a tight ball of cells surrounded by the glycoprotein zona pellucida.

Mucoid — Resembling mucus.

Multiparous — Having born two or more offspring in separate pregnancies.

Fetal mummy — Desiccated fetal remnants.

Naso-gastric tube — Tube placed into the horse's nostrils, through the pharynx, into the esophagus, and down into the stomach. Used to administer large volumes of oral medications and intestinal lubricants directly into the stomach of a horse. It is also used as a means of providing an escape route for built up ingest and gas from the stomach in horses which are colicking. Horses cannot normally vomit, and severe build up of gas and ingesta can result in a gastric rupture.

Necrosis — Death of tissue.

Negative energy balance — When the metabolic demands of the animal for energy are greater than what is provided by its dietary intake.

Neonate — A newborn.

Neuroendocrine response — A reflex arc that involves a nervous system component and a endocrine system component.

Neurological — Signs related to the normal or abnormal workings of the nervous system.

Nurse mare — A mare used as a foster mother to adopt a foal and nurse and rear it when its own mother cannot do so.

Oocyte — A cell in the ovary, derived from the primordial germ cells, that becomes the haploid progenitor "female" cell that when fertilized by a male's spermatozoa will go on to form a new individual.

Open mare — Mare which is not pregnant because she was not bred during the previous breeding season.

Ovaries — The paired female gonads, contain the oocytes and produce estrogen (ovarian follicle) and progesterone (ovarian corpus luteum).

Oviducts — Site of fertilization, tubular structures that receive and support the ovulated oocyte from the ovary, transport it to the site of fertilization, then nourish the early embryo and transport it to the uterus. Likewise the oviducts support and transport spermatozoa from the uterus to the site of fertilization.

Palpation — Examination by touch or pressure of the hand over an organ or area of the body, as a diagnostic aid. In mares the reproductive tract is examined by palpating it through the mare's rectal wall.

Parturition — The act of giving birth.

Pasture stocking rates — Refers to the number of horses grazed or housed on an acre of pasture.

Pathogen — Any microorganism or substance capable of causing disease.

Patent urachus — Failure of the umbilical urachus to close completely after birth, resulting in urine being dribbled directly from the bladder through the umbilical cord remnant. The presence of a patent urachus also provides bacteria ready access to the foal's bladder and bloodstream.

Pathology — The study of disease; term also used to refer to the mechanisms and/or results of the development of a disease condition.

Perineal body — The connective and soft tissue layers present between the rectum and the vagina.

Perineum — The area between and immediately surrounding the external genitalia and the anus.

Peristalsis — The wave-like contraction and relaxation of the intestinal tract as it moves ingesta down its length.

Peritonitis — Inflammation of the peritoneal (abdominal) cavity and lining usually as a result of chemical irritation or infection.

Physiological — Denoting the various normal processes of a living organism.

Pitting edema — Edematous swelling (usually under the skin) that holds an indentation mark if pressed with a fingertip.

Placenta — Membranes of fetal origin that provide a point of attachment and exchange of nutrients, oxygen, and waste products between the maternal and fetal bloodstreams in the pregnant uterus. The placenta also functions as an endocrine organ and produces an number of different hormones that help to regulate pregnancy.

Placentitis — Inflammation of the placenta usually due to a fungal or bacterial organism.

Pneumonia — Inflammation of the lungs caused by viruses, bacteria, or chemical agents and foreign bodies.

Pneumovagina — Air-filled vaginal cavity usually as a direct result of aspiration of air through the vulvar lips in mares which are predisposed to this condition due to poor vulvar and/or perineal conformation.

Postpartum — After birth.

Primary corpus luteum — Corpus luteum that formed from the ovulatory follicle that resulted in the pregnancy.

Progestagens — Hormones produced by the equine placenta which has similar effects as progesterone and which are responsible for maintaining the equine pregnancy after approximately day 120 to 150 of the gestation.

Progesterone — Ovarian steroid produced by the corpus luteum which stimulates changes in the uterus to support and maintain a developing pregnancy; maintains the uterus in a quiescent state, and keeps the cervix tightly closed.

Prolactin — Hormone produced by the pituitary gland that promotes and maintains lactation and is also thought to be responsible for stimulating maternal behavior.

Prostaglandin — Hormone produced by a number of tissues and liberated during a number of pathologic conditions, causes uterine contractions and destruction of a mature corpus luteum.

Pyometra — Rare condition in the mare in which there is a large accumulation of pus in the uterus. Abnormalities in the mare's cervix after trauma or otherwise that do not permit drainage of fluid and debris from the uterine lumen are thought to predispose a mare to this condition.

Recrudescence — A return of a morbid process after a dormant or inactive period.

Rectovaginal fistula — Formation of a communicating opening in the tissues between the rectum and the vagina secondary to trauma during foaling. Chronic fecal contamination of the vagina results in infertility due to resultant vaginitis, cervicitis, and endometritis.

Red bag delivery — Premature placental separation during foaling in which the allantochorion fails to rupture and the chorionic surface begins to detach from the uterus. There is no "breaking of the waters" and the red chorion appears at the vulva rather than the white amnion. Premature separation of the placenta threatens to disrupt the foal's oxygen supply prior to its delivery, and it is vital that the allantochorion be ruptured manually to deter any further separation and that the foal be delivered as quickly as possible.

Retained placenta — A term used to describe any placenta that has not been expelled in its entirety within three hours of the delivery of the foal.

Rhinopneumonitis — A herpesvirus infection with EHV I or IV resulting in upper respiratory symptoms in affected horses. Also used to refer to EHV I in terms of causing equine abortions.

Secondary corpora lutea — Corpora lutea that form on the ovaries of a pregnant mare after day 40 of gestation in response to ECG secretion by the endometrial cups. These secondary corpora lutea serve as back up progesterone production to the primary corpus luteum.

Septicemia — Systemic disease caused by the presence of pathogenic organisms in the body; sometimes used to refer to infections where pathogenic organisms and their toxins have gained access to the infected individual's bloodstream.

Seronegative — Term referring to the absence of any detectable antibodies against a disease agent.

Serous — Resembling serum; frequently used to refer to an amber, watery, sticky discharge.

Shedder — Term used to refer to an infected individual who is releasing an infectious agent into the environment.

Short cycle — Term used to describe the premature termination of the diestrus period and the mare's hastened return to estrus.

Singleton pregnancy — Pregnancy in which the mare is carrying only one viable embryo or fetus.

Specific gravity — The ratio of the mass of any substance (usually liquid) to the mass of an equal volume of another substance (usually distilled water).

Spermatozoa — Specialized male, haploid progenitor cell derived from the primordial germ cells and produced in the male's testicles which combines with an oocyte during fertilization to form a new individual.

Strangulating intestinal colic — Pathological intestinal lesion in which the blood supply of a portion of the intestinal tract has been cut off due to the intestine twisting back on itself along its mesentery; a lipoma wrapping itself around the intestine, thrombosis of the mesenteric blood supply secondary to a larval migration, etc.

Subclinical — Denoting the phase of a disease prior to the manifestation of symptoms.

Symbiotic relationship — The living together in intimate association of two dissimilar organisms where both parties benefit from the relationship.

Systemic — Relating to or affecting the entire body.

Tail head — The root of the tail where the tail emerges from the base of the spine.

Tease — Process of exposing a mare to a male to see whether she is receptive to being bred.

Teaser — A male horse (stallion or gelding with good libido) used to stimulate a mare to see if she is receptive to being bred.

Theriogenology — The study of reproduction.

Thirty Day Heat — Term used to refer to the first estrus period following the foal heat which usually occurs approximately 30 days after the mare has foaled.

Titer — The measured level of antibodies in the blood against a given antigen.

Torsion — The act of turning or twisting of a structure around its long axis.

Toxemia — A condition caused by the presence in the blood of poisonous products of bacteria formed at a local site of infection.

Transabdominal — Across the abdominal wall.

Transvaginal — Across the vaginal wall; also used to refer to entering the cervix and the uterus by way of the vagina.

Trimester — One third of the length of gestation.

Trophoblast cells — The outer layer of embryonic cells forming the wall of the blastocyst. Eventually they go on to form the placenta and not the embryo proper. The embryo itself arises from the cells forming the embryonic disc of the blastocyst.

Tubular tone — Term used to describe the quality of the tone of the pregnant uterus. The uterine horns are quite pronounced on palpation and maintain their tubular shape and orientation as the uterus is gently lifted and manipulated.

Twin reduction — Term that loosely applies to any one of a number of techniques by which one member of a twin pregnancy is destroyed leaving only a single viable embryo or fetus to carry on till term.

Twitch — A restraint device that is applied to a horse's upper lip.

Ultrasound — Process by which sound waves are generated by a crystal and pass into tissues where they are reflected back in different intensities depending upon the density of the reflecting tissue or medium. A transducer receives the reflected sound waves and converts the various intensities into an image that can be used to interpret the structure of the tissues being examined. Ultrasound waves do not pass through air or bone, but readily pass through fluids.

Umbilical cord — The structure connecting the placenta with the fetus.

Unilateral twins — Twin embryos which fixate and implant side by side in the same uterine horn.

Urine Pooling — Condition in which urine runs forward into the vagina during urination and collects in the floor of the cranial vagina adjacent to and sometimes submerging the cervix. The presence of the urine results in a chronic vaginitis, cervicitis, and endometritis due to the chemical irritation of the urine. Urine pooling can occur secondary to poor, sloping vaginal and pelvic conformations, injury, and/or relaxation and stretching of the vaginal structures during estrus, late pregnancy, and/or post foaling.

Uterine cytology — Examination of the cells and secretions in the uterine lumen for signs of inflammation and infection.

Uterine glands — Glands in the endometrium that produce the histotroph.

Uterine involution — Postpartum process during which the uterus returns to its pre-pregnant size and shape and the endometrial lining recovers and regenerates to be able to support a new pregnancy. A very rapid process in the normal mare.

Uterine lavage — The act of flushing the uterine lumen with fluid in order to retrieve an embryo or flush out accumulated fluid and inflammatory debris.

Uterus — Muscular and glandular organ of pregnancy; in the mare it is a T-shaped organ made up of two uterine horns (left and right) which form the crossbar of the "T" and a uterine body which forms the base of the "T."

Uveitis — Inflammation of the inner structures of the eye (also referred to as periodic opthalmia or moon blindness).

Vaginal speculum — Instrument used to view the interior of the vaginal lumen and the external cervical os.

Varicose veins — Abnormally dilated and tortuous blood vessels; in mares varicose veins sometimes form and become prominent in the vaginal or vestibular walls during pregnancy and sometimes during estrus. These veins have a tendency to bleed and can result in a bloody vulvar discharge.

Venereal — Related to or resulting from sexual intercourse.

Vestibule — Term related to the short tubular cavity between the vulva and the vagina.

Vestibular vaginal junction/sphincter — Soft tissue narrowing that separates the vestibule from the vagina at the level of the back border of the floor of the pelvis. Site where the hymen is found if it is intact. One of the three barriers between the outside environment and the uterine lumen (the other two are the vulvar lips and the cervix).

Viable — Alive.

Vulva — The external female genitalia, the opening to the female urogenital tract bordered by the vulvar lips or labia.

Waxing — The accumulation of a waxy secretion on the mare's teat endings typically when she is within 24 hours of foaling.

White blood cells — Cells in the blood stream that are part of the body's immunologic defense; neutrophil white blood cells will leave the blood stream and migrate to areas of cellular damage and infection as part of the cellular defense mechanisms.

White muscle disease — Muscle cell deterioration and death due to body deficiencies in selenium and or vitamin E; can result in weakness and even death of the neonate if the cardiac muscle is severely affected.

Winking — Act by which the mare everts and briefly exteriorizes her clitoris so that it is visible. Mares commonly will do this after urinating and the behavior is exaggerated and also seen in direct response to stimulation by a teaser when a mare is in estrus or heat.

Wry Muzzle — A congenital deformity in which a foal's muzzle is twisted to one side. In severe cases the misshapen head can cause a dystocia.

Yolk sac — The highly vascular umbilical vesicle enveloping the nutritive yolk of an early embryo.

Zona pelucida — The glycoprotein coat that surrounds the embryo from the zygote through the morula and on through the early blastocyst stage.

Zoonotic — Any disease transmissible from animals to humans.

Zygote — The initial, single, diploid-fertilized cell formed by the union of the oocyte and spermatozoa

RECOMMENDED READINGS

Lay texts

Cable, C. *Understanding The Foal*. Lexington, Ky: The Blood-Horse Publications, Inc. 1998

Evans, W.; Borton, A., Hintz, H., and Van Vleck, D. *The Horse*. 2 ed. San Francisco: W. H. Freeman 1990.

Schweizer, C. *Understanding Breeding Management*. Lexington, Ky: The Blood-Horse Publications, Inc. 1998

Taylor, J. *Joe Taylor's Complete Guide to Breeding and Raising Racehorses*. Neenah, Wisc: Russell Meerdink Company, Ltd. 1993

Briggs, K. *Understanding Equine Nutrition*. Lexington, Ky: The Blood-Horse Publications, Inc. 1998

Veterinary texts

McKinnon, AO. and Voss, JL. *Equine Reproduction*. Philadelphia: Lea &Febiger. 1993

Robinson, E. *Current Therapy in Equine Medicine*. Vol. 3 & 4. Philadelphia: W.B. Saunders Company. 1992, 1997.

Youngquist, RS. *Current Therapy in Large Animal Theriogenology*. Philadelphia: W.B. Saunders Company. 1997

Picture Credits

CHAPTER 1
Barry Ball, DVM, 13; The Blood-Horse, 16.

CHAPTER 2
Barry Ball, 22; Christine M. Schweizer, 29; The Blood-Horse, 32.

CHAPTER 3
Anne M. Eberhardt, 34, 36.

CHAPTER 4
Anne M. Eberhardt, 38, 41, 42.

CHAPTER 5
Anne M. Eberhardt, 50, 52, 60.

CHAPTER 6
Anne M. Eberhardt, 62, 72, 76; Christine M. Schweizer, 64, 65, 68, 70;
Robert Hillman, DVM, 65-67, 73; Barry Ball, 69; Barrie Britt, DVM, 69;
Katherine Houpt, DVM, 71.

CHAPTER 7
Skip Dickstein, 78.

CHAPTER 8
Christina Cable, DVM, 93; Barry Ball, 96; Anne M. Eberhardt, 99, 101.

CHAPTER 9
Anne M. Eberhardt, 106, 116; Barbara D. Livingston, 109; John Wyatt, 115.

CHAPTER 10
Anne M. Eberhardt, 122, 126.

EDITOR — JACQUELINE DUKE
COVER/BOOK DESIGN — SUZANNE C. DEPP
ILLUSTRATIONS — ROBIN PETERSON
COVER PHOTO — SUZIE PICOU OLDHAM

About the Author

Christine M. Schweizer, DVM grew up in Elmont, Long Island, N.Y. and spent much of her youth working with Thoroughbred racehorses at Belmont, Aqueduct, and Saratoga racetracks. She received her bachelor's degree in animal science from Cornell University and her DVM from the New York State College of Veterinary Medicine at Cornell. After graduating, she spent a year in a mixed

Christine Schweizer, DVM

animal practice at the Cazenovia Animal Hospital in Cazenovia, N.Y., then entered an equine medicine and surgery internship at the Rochester Equine Clinic in Rochester, N.H.

After completing her internship, Dr. Schweizer returned to Cornell University's Veterinary College to complete a residencey program in theriogenology (reproductive medicine). She spent part of her internship at Hagyard-Davidson-McGee equine hospital in Lexington, Ky., under Drs. Walter Zent and John Steiner. Dr. Schweizer sat her specialty boards in 1995 and became a Diplomate in the American College of Theriogenologists. She is currently on faculty at The New York State College of Veterinary Medicine, where she is a lecturer and clinician in the small and large animal clinics, and participates in managing the Section of Theriogenology's equine herd and clinical equine breeding services. Outside of the equine breeding season, Dr. Schweizer enjoys riding and working with her own horses and breeding and showing her Boxer dogs. She lives in Ithaca with her husband, Dr. Joseph Wilder, and their two young children.